STIEG AND ME

STIEG AND ME

Memories of my life
with Stieg Larsson

EVA GABRIELSSON

WITH MARIE-FRANÇOISE COLOMBANI
TRANSLATED FROM THE FRENCH BY LINDA COVERDALE

First published in Great Britain in 2011
by Orion Books

1 3 5 7 9 10 8 6 4 2

English Translation © 2011 Linda Coverdale

Original title: *Millénium, Stieg et moi*
Original publisher: Actes Sud, 2011
© 2011 Actes Sud

Photo illustrations from the personal collection of Eva Gabrielsson

A CIP catalogue record for this book is available from the British Library.

ISBN: 978 1 4091 4134 1

Typeset by Input Data Services Ltd, Bridgwater, Somerset
Printed and bound in the UK by CPI Mackays, Chatham ME5 8TD

The Orion Publishing Group's policy is to use papers that are natural,
renewable and recyclable and made from wood grown in sustainable forests.
The logging and manufacturing processes are expected to conform to
environmental regulations of the country of origin.

Orion Books

Orion Publishing Group Ltd
Orion House
5 Upper Saint Martin's Lane
London, WC2H 9EA

An Hachette UK Company

www.orionbooks.co.uk

Till alla Er som höll mig när jag inte höll ihop själv.
Och till Er som stannade kvar efteråt.

To all those who supported me when I faltered.
And to those who are standing by me still.

—EG

Contents

Foreword

YES, THERE is a mystery behind *The Millennium Trilogy*. And secrets, too. As in the parable of Plato's Cave, Stieg Larsson's crime novels allow only a certain reality to appear, and the reality that remains hidden within them is rich in stories that open endlessly onto still more stories. The trilogy is filled with signs, some of which are drawn from everyday life while others, strangely powerful, link Stieg Larsson and Eva Gabrielsson, his companion of thirty-two years, to worlds distinctly their own: science fiction, the Bible, Scandinavian mythology, espionage, the battle against right-wing extremism, the struggle for human rights. . . .

Only Eva Gabrielsson can shed an intimate light on the *Millennium* novels, which in her telling become much more than the crime fiction saga known throughout the world.

The trilogy is an allegory of the individual's eternal fight for justice and morality, the values for which Stieg Larsson fought until the day he died. To Eva Gabrielsson, these books are the reflection of a shared life and love, but also the embodiment of terrible events. The first and most dramatic of these, of course, was the sudden loss of Stieg. Felled by a heart attack at the age of fifty soon after delivering his manuscripts to his publisher, Stieg never witnessed the immense success of his creation. And what happened next was sordid. Because domestic unions between unmarried childless couples are not legally recognized in Sweden, Eva was deprived of all of her inheritance from her partner and for a time even feared she would be evicted from their small apartment, only half of which she owned. Another distressing development for Eva was the growth of a huge "Stieg Larsson industry," the complete antithesis of everything he stood for: TV series, films, books by false friends, all kinds of rumors. . . . The real Stieg Larsson—the militant, the feminist, the journalist, the autodidact of a vast and eclectic culture—gradually disappeared, leaving the blockbuster author alone in the spotlight.

From beginning to end, Stieg's life was a true saga, and Eva, a major character in that intimate novel, has decided to give us a few keys to his roman à clef. This plainspoken, straightforward woman, as loyal and idealistic as Stieg himself, does not make compromises. Those who know her know this well. Come what may, her friends can count on her, just as they could count on her companion. The rest have been left behind on the path of betrayal, as Stieg would have done.

Today Eva is fighting to obtain control over Larsson's literary estate. She is doing it for him, because he would have hated more than anything else to see his early writings, his articles against racism, his books about the far right, and his *Millennium Trilogy* milked for profits. If Eva's request is granted, she will clear up the mystery shrouding the fourth novel in the series, for she has followed its genesis closely, just as she did with the first three volumes. Those of us in love with the trilogy may therefore still hope one day to rejoin our heroes, and as for the enemies of Lisbeth Salander and Mikael Blomkvist—let them tremble, for this fourth book will be entitled *The Vengeance of God*. And they should know this: Eva, tempered in the fires of adversity, is poised to write the final words of their fate and lead a dance on their graves.

MARIE-FRANÇOISE COLOMBANI

"THERE ARE THINGS I WANT YOU TO KNOW"
ABOUT STIEG LARSSON AND ME

Speaking of Coffee

PEOPLE OFTEN ask me if the Swedish drink as much coffee as the characters do in *The Millennium Trilogy*. Well, we drink a lot of it indeed, given that Finland is the only country in the world that consumes more coffee than we do. And if I had to single out just one thing in common between Stieg Larsson and Mikael Blomkvist, it would surely be their impressive daily quota of coffee.

Stieg and I shared this addiction, which dates from our childhood. (Stieg's grandmother began giving him coffee openly when he was five, when children ordinarily drink milk; my grandmother did the same with me, but more discreetly, since my mother was still around.) Coffee was for both of us an extraordinary remedy for all kinds of misfortunes great or small. Synonymous with intimacy, conviviality, hospitality, it accompanied our moments of happiness as well as our long, long conversations with each other or friends. In the course of our thirty-two years together, I think we were largely responsible for the Swedish coffee industry's handsome profits! Although we experimented with every possible way of preparing the brew, we always fell back on percolated coffee. In our home, a coffeepot sat permanently on the stove.

◫

THESE DAYS, I don't fix coffee for myself anymore. It's silly to fill only half a coffeepot. Besides, the empty half means that Stieg will never again look at me over the rim of his cup, his eyes twinkling with curiosity, like a child who's just been given a present. Never again will I hear him say, "So, tell me: What did you do today? What new things have you discovered?"

In *The Millennium Trilogy*, Lisbeth Salander sometimes breaks off a discussion with Mikael Blomkvist by saying, "I'll think about it." The first time I read that, I burst out laughing! Whenever Stieg and I reached an impasse during a serious argument because I wouldn't adopt his point of view, I always wound up saying those same words. They meant that it was time to move on to a more neutral and pleasant conversation, so at this signal, one of us would immediately get up to go make a pot of coffee, and we'd be friends again.

Nowadays I never drink coffee at home by myself.
I've switched to tea.

◉

THIS BOOK . . . I wish I hadn't had to write it. It talks
about Stieg, and our life together, but also about my life
without him.

A heart attack took him from me on November 9, 2004.
An accursed day for me, and for many others in the past as
well, to whom it brought tremendous tragedy. I'm thinking
of November 9, 1938: Kristallnacht, the "Night of Broken
Glass," when the Nazis drew one step closer to the Final
Solution by attacking their Jewish fellow citizens. Stieg always commemorated Kristallnacht by participating in public events. On that evening of November 9, 2004, he was to
have given a lecture at the headquarters of the ABF
(Arbetarnas Bildningsförbund), the Workers' Educational
Association, in Stockholm.

Because of my work as an architect, I was not with Stieg
when he died but in the province of Dalarna, in central
Sweden. Would it have made any difference if I had been
there? I'll never know, obviously, but I like to believe so.
Whenever we were together, that communion affected our
lives profoundly.

◉

"*MILLENNIUM* STIEG," the author of best-selling crime thrillers, was born in July 2005 with the publication of the first novel in his trilogy. Since then there have been feature films and TV movies.

And yet, the trilogy is only one episode in Stieg's journey through this world, and it certainly isn't his life's work.

The Stieg of the "*Millennium* industry" doesn't interest me.

The one I care about is my life partner and my ally in everything. The man I loved deeply, with whom I went through life for thirty-two years. An affectionate man, generous, funny, enthusiastic, committed. . . . The journalist, the feminist, the militant. The love of my life.

When I lost him, a huge part of me was lost with him.

◙

THAT STIEG was born on August 15, 1954. . . .

Early Days

IN *THE Girl with the Dragon Tattoo*, the novel that opens *The Millennium Trilogy*, Mikael Blomkvist discovers a photo taken during the Children's Day Parade in Hedeby, the oldest neighborhood in the small town of Hedestad, on the day Harriet Vanger disappeared. Seeking information about that day to help him understand what might have frightened the teenager away, he hunts for the tourist couple who photographed the parade forty years earlier. His research takes him into northern Sweden, first to Norsjö, then to Bjursele, in Västerbotten County. Why there? For most Swedes, those are godforsaken places at the back of beyond, but Stieg knew them well. It was there that he went as a baby in 1955 to live with his maternal grandparents. His father and mother,

Erland Larsson and Vivianne Boström, were too young to bring him up properly, and they left to live 600 miles away in the south. In 1957 they moved again to Umeå (pronounced Umio), a small city 125 miles southeast of Norsjö.

Writing about Norsjö and Bjursele was Stieg's way of paying homage to the small community of people there who gave him the best moments of his youth. And a way of thanking them for the values they instilled in him.

▣

STIEG LIVED with his grandparents in a small wooden house on the edge of a forest. Their home had a kitchen and one other room, without water, electricity, or an indoor toilet. This kind of house is typical of the Swedish countryside and its family farms, and in those days, when the next generation took over the farm, the old folks would "retire" to such a place. The walls of Stieg's grandparents' house were poorly insulated, and the joints between the planks were probably crammed with sawdust in the old style. The kitchen woodstove on which his grandmother cooked the meals was the only source of heat. In the winter, the temperature outside could drop to as low as -35 degrees Celsius, with—at most—thirty minutes of daylight, and Stieg used to ski cross-country to the village school in the moonlight. Prompted by his natural curiosity, he tirelessly explored the surrounding forests, lakes, and trails, hoping to meet other people and catch glimpses of animals, too. Life was tough where he lived, so it took plenty of ingenuity to survive, but such an environment breeds hardy individuals, self-reliant, resourceful, generous folks who can be counted on in a pinch. Like Stieg.

According to Stieg, his maternal grandfather, Severin, was an anti-Nazi communist who was imprisoned in an internment camp during World War II. After the war, such militants were not exactly welcomed back into society. Even at the time, people didn't want to talk about this period in Swedish history, and what happened then is still not common knowledge today. In 1955, Severin quit his job in a factory and left Skelleftehamn—where Stieg was born—to move into that small wooden house with his wife and their baby grandson. To support his little family, Severin repaired bikes and engines and did odd jobs on the local farms. Stieg adored going hunting and fishing with him. At the beginning of *The Girl with the Dragon Tattoo*, Mikael Blomkvist accepts an offer from Henrik Vanger, Harriet Vanger's uncle, to move into the guest house not far from Hedestad. It's the middle of winter, and he describes the "ice roses that formed on the inside of the windows": they were the same ones that used to fascinate Stieg in his grandparents' home, roses that grew from vapor in the family's breath and the water always boiling on the stove. He never forgot those magnificent visions, or the cold he could describe from personal experience. His childhood was a hard one, but it was full of joy and affection.

In black-and-white family snapshots, a little boy smiles between two grown-ups who've been having fun disguising themselves for the camera. Those two taught Stieg that nothing is impossible in this life. And that chasing after money is contemptible. His grandfather had an old Ford Anglia, the motor of which he'd probably repaired thanks to his skills as a mechanic and handyman, and this very car, with AC on its license plate for Västerbotten, is the one Mikael must track down during his search for Harriet Vanger. To write his trilogy, Stieg used a thousand such small details taken from life. From his life, from mine, and from ours.

▣

IN DECEMBER 1962, Severin Boström, Stieg's grandfather, died suddenly of a heart attack at the age of fifty-six (as did his daughter, Stieg's mother, in 1991). Six months later his widow, unable to stay on in that isolated house with her grandchild, moved with him to the area around Skellefteå, in Västerbotten County, where Stieg would later visit her every summer until she died, in 1968.

Severin's death brought Stieg's happy, carefree world to an abrupt end. He was not quite nine years old when he rejoined his parents in Umeå. In 1957 Erland and Vivianne had had another son, Joakim, and they had married in 1958. Stieg barely knew them anymore. He used to speak often about his maternal grandparents but rarely about his parents, although some very close friends of his grandparents have told me that his mama, Vivianne, did go to see him several times when he was very little. In the autumn of 1963, when Stieg began attending elementary school in Umeå, his life changed completely. He found the urban environment foreign, even hostile.

He was used to living in a house out in the middle of nature, coming and going in perfect freedom, but from then on he lived shut up in a tiny apartment in the middle of town, and this switch from countryside to asphalt was painful for him. Stieg's parents worked all day and were often absent, whereas his grandparents had always been available. The rhythm of life grew stricter, more cramped, governed by regular hours.

Stieg's first name was originally spelled without an *e*, and I'm not sure when he added the extra letter because he was already "Stieg" when I met him. There was another Stig Larsson in Umeå, and the story goes that they flipped a coin one day to see who would change his name. What I do know is that after Stieg received an impressive number of letters from the village library demanding the return of books checked out by the other Stig, he decided it was time for a new name. (And I'm always amused when people trot out similar anecdotes about him as if they'd been there at the time or Stieg had personally told them what happened, when I'm the only one who knew those particular stories, which they've gleaned from the interviews I've given.)

When he was seventeen, Stieg moved out of his family's apartment into a small studio in the basement of the building where they lived. Beyond the fact that he wasn't too happy, I don't know what really went on during all those years. I have the distinct impression, though, that it was from that time on that he stopped taking care of himself and began neglecting his health. As if all that simply weren't important anymore. As if *he* weren't important, either to himself or to others.

Aside from the all too rare times when we went sailing, Stieg, like Mikael Blomkvist, didn't go in much for sports, ate indiscriminately, smoked, and I've already said he drank too much coffee. Which, given the stressful life he led, doubtless contributed to his premature death.

After I met Stieg, in 1972, he returned only once to his childhood home, in the autumn of 1996.

Norsjö and Bjursele are in Västerbotten County, where my brother, sister, and I own about eighteen acres of woodlands that have been in our family for generations. In the 1990s, Stieg and I went up there twice to clear some brush. The second time, in 1996, we spent several days working hard among the snakes and biting flies, but it felt good to get out of our offices and do some manual labor. And when we'd finished clearing the undergrowth, we went to see his grandparents' little house with some neighbors of ours from the nearby village of Önnesmark, since they were curious to know more about Stieg's childhood days.

The house was shut up tight, so Stieg pressed his face to the window. Nothing had changed.

"It's just like it was back then! Look, that's where I slept, with Grandfather. And it's still the same old stove! I remember it was stone cold in the morning, and we would all freeze."

He revisited every square yard, every tree, every stone, every hill. . . . Slowly, his memories came back to him. He was deeply moved and I, I was stunned. I had never seen him like that. Even his voice was transformed: it was warmer, more solemn, and he was speaking so softly, almost in a whisper. Spurred on by our questions, he told story after story. When the time came to leave, he kept saying, "One moment more, just a moment more . . ." He could not tear himself away from the place.

It was getting later and later. Then he turned to me, pleadingly, and asked, "Eva, couldn't we buy the house?"

"But dear, it's more than six hundred miles from Stockholm, it's too far away! We wouldn't be able to come very often. And since we haven't enough money or time to spend here, the place would just go to ruin."

Then, with infinite sadness, he murmured, "But . . . it's all I have." He seemed overwhelmed by the fathomless sorrow of a child, as if, drawn more than thirty years back into the past, he were once more being torn away from his roots. We all stood there for a long time, silent, lost in our own thoughts. Then Stieg said, as if giving up, "It's impossible." And we left, with heavy hearts.

I'd taken lots of photos of that little house, which I later made into a collage that I framed and gave to Stieg. He was so pleased with it that he hung it on the wall over our bed.

WE OFTEN talked about that trip as if it had been a magical moment. In the summer of 2004, after he'd delivered the three *Millennium* volumes to the publisher, we made heaps of plans for the future. We used to imagine—among other things, and I'll say more about this later—"our little writing cottage," which we wanted to build on an island. Stieg and I would make drawings of it, each off on our own, and then compare our sketches, sitting side by side on our *kökssoffa*, which is a wooden settee with an upholstered seat. (Many Swedish kitchens have one for seating and as an extra bed, but our settee was in the living room, since the kitchen was too small.) I often studied Stieg's snapshots of his grandparents' wooden house, and I wanted to surprise him by using the same entryway and blue-and-white doors in our cottage.

Our Mamas

PEOPLE HAVE pointed out to me that, aside from Mikael Blomkvist's sister, there are no conventional mothers in *The Millennium Trilogy*, or any traditional families, either. Lisbeth Salander's mother remained a passive victim of her husband Zala's violence and was unable to protect her child, which leads to tragedy. Brain-damaged by his beatings, she ends her days in a clinic where she dies relatively young. As for the women of the Vanger family, the worst of them are bad mothers, like Isabella Vanger, Harriet and Martin's mother, who knew that her husband was abusing their son (who was himself raping his sister), but she "paid no attention to all that." At best, these women are uncaring mothers, or they don't have children, like Erika Berger.

When I think about this, I don't believe it's an accident. Stieg and I grew up motherless, since we were both brought up by our grandparents. But the most attentive and affectionate of grandmothers, as ours were, cannot replace a child's mama.

Being raised by that older generation also meant that in a way we were growing up in the nineteenth century, in a time untouched by modern mores. We were taught old-fashioned values, a strict and sometimes severe morality. In our homes, an honorable reputation did not depend on money and success, but on integrity. Once given, a person's word was sacred. These rules were inviolable.

Stieg and I were alike in many, many ways, especially in our thinking and our reactions to things. We found that funny, but it was hardly surprising, after all, since we shared the same background.

I was born on November 17, 1953, in Lövånger, about sixty miles north of Umeå, in the Skellefteå Municipality of Västerbotten County. I was the oldest of three children born a little more than a year apart. Our parents separated when I was seven, and we children stayed on the family farm with our father and paternal grandparents. Father hadn't wanted to become a farmer, and although he'd left school at the age of thirteen, he'd still managed to become a journalist at a regional daily newspaper. My parents had married for love and could have spent their lives together, if only they had lived in the city. Gudrun, my mother, was a secondary school graduate and had worked as a secretary in a metallurgy factory before her marriage. For a time, my grandmother had hoped that her daughter-in-law would help out on the farm, but she soon saw how unfit for country life Mama was in her lipstick, high heels, and tailored suits. Such frills were completely useless, in Grandmother's eyes, whereas I thought Mama was lively and pretty. My parents' divorce was a harrowing experience, and their two families also split apart during the ordeal. My father obtained custody of his children, which was a rare thing at the time, by showing that he had a job, a place to live, and that my paternal grandparents would look after us. I also think the fact that my father belonged to the Liberal People's Party and knew influential people in the area weighed heavily in his favor.

So my mother went to live on her own in Stockholm, where she studied and became a nurse. In thirty-one years, I saw her only six times. She never remarried. My father died in 1977, and my mother died of cancer in December 1992, during the Christmas holidays. Although my paternal grandmother, a kind and honest woman, felt that my father had made a mistake in marrying my mother, she would never, ever, have tried to prevent her from seeing us again. So I just don't know what went on in Mama's head. I think she was a sensitive and psychologically fragile person. She suffered cruelly at being separated from her children, but we were far away and she hadn't much money, so what could she do? When she went away in 1961, my siblings and I lost not just our mama, but our entire maternal family, forever.

And then I felt absolutely abandoned, just as Stieg did when he was separated from his grandparents in 1962.

◨

STIEG AND my grandmother got along wonderfully from the moment they met. She used to say that he was "a good man," while he thought she was "fabulous." I must say that she was a determined woman who knew what she wanted. So did her father: after sailing the seven seas for more than twenty-one years, he became a farmer so that he could marry his beloved young fiancée. My grandmother had a way of saying, "Well, here's what I think," that gave us all pause before we embarked on something. The subtext was obvious: "You, you do what you want, but you'll be responsible for whatever happens."

When I met Stieg, his mama, Vivianne, became my "substitute" mother. She was another woman of strong will. And like my grandmother, she was the one who ran her family. I really admired her. She managed a ready-to-wear store, but her ambition was to change society, and to the amazement of the local political bigwigs, she was elected to the city council on the Social Democratic ticket. "Nothing mysterious about it," she explained with a grin. "What with all the customers traipsing through the shop, everyone in town knew who I was!" And since I'm an architect, when Vivianne joined the municipal urban planning commission, the two of us had one more thing to share.

Stieg and Vivianne were very much alike, and anything they did was done with wholehearted commitment. He was fond of her, but not in the way one loves a mother; it was more as if he felt comfortably close to her. And he treated his father and brother as if they were his foster family. After we moved to Stockholm in 1977, we didn't often travel the six hundred or so miles to Umeå. In Önnesmark, a village in my native locality of Lövånger, Stieg's parents had a vacation home (coincidentally enough, the house had been built by my paternal great-uncle), and they loaned the place to us a few times during the summer months. In the 1980s, we also spent a few Christmases in Umeå with Stieg's parents, but most of the time we spent holidays with my family: Christmas, Easter, and Midsummer's Day— which we Swedes celebrate lavishly, feasting on seasonal foods, putting up decorations of greenery and wildflowers, and dancing to folk music around a huge maypole. We even considered making Midsummer's Day our national holiday!

Then Vivianne got breast cancer, and in August of 1991, on her way home after a treatment session at the hospital, she suffered an aneurysm. We immediately flew up from Stockholm to be with her. She was unconscious, but I held her hand and told her softly about Stieg, our plans, what we were working on, as if everything were fine. I felt that she could hear me. The next day, she died. She had waited for us. Just as my mother would do the following year. She too had had breast cancer, and then she was diagnosed with lung cancer, which she fought with a tenacity that astonished everyone in the clinic for palliative care where she was hospitalized. I can still see her sitting on the balcony, wrapped in a blanket, smoking and coughing. My brother and I began taking turns at her bedside, but my sister, who lived in London, was unable to join us before Christmas. So my mother hung on. At the end of December, with her three children gathered around her, she died. So our two mamas both chose the moment when they would let go.

Not Stieg. He was ambushed, taken by surprise.

◙

AFTER WE bought our apartment on the large island of Södermalm—a district in central Stockholm—in 1991, we celebrated all our holidays in the capital with my brother and sister. Erland, Stieg's father, would come to the city from time to time with his new companion, Gun, and then we'd have coffee or dinner together at a café or restaurant, depending on our various schedules. Erland often urged Stieg to come see his brother, if only for a short while whenever we drove up to clear brush from the forest around the small cabin I shared with my siblings in Önnesmark, but there was almost no bond between the two brothers. This is why we did not attend Joakim's wedding or any of the family birthday celebrations. Stieg would sidestep the subject with Erland by explaining that his work kept him fairly busy. Still, I do remember a few times when we were passing through Umeå and had coffee with Joakim and his family just to please Erland. Joakim clearly doesn't remember all this, as he has told the media about having quite strong ties with Stieg. In thirty years, Joakim came to our home only twice: once at the end of the

1970s, and again when Stieg died. Stieg and I always saw a lot of my brother and sister, on the other hand, because— after I had lost both parents and grandparents and no longer had any relationship with my mother's family, and because Stieg did not feel close to his remaining blood relatives—my brother and sister were our real family.

Meeting

IN THE autumn of 1972, my sister Britt and I attended a meeting in support of the Front National de Libération in Vietnam (the FNL) at the Mimer School in Umeå. It was the first time I'd ever gone to anything like that. My father used to vote for the Liberal People's Party, but that was the extent of his involvement, while I considered myself to be a reasonably politically aware person, and that was enough for me. The Vietnam War had upset and sickened me ever since I was fourteen, however, and now that I'd finished high school, I felt it was time for me to take a serious interest in something other than studies and diplomas.

A tall, thin guy with dark brown hair, warm eyes, and a broad, cheerful smile was greeting everyone arriving for the meeting with an energetic "Welcome!" It was Stieg. He was barely eighteen, while I was almost nineteen. He asked Britt and me lots of questions, and when he learned that we lived in Haga, a neighborhood in Umeå, he immediately recruited us for the team he himself would be leading. Later he told me that he'd seen his chance and pounced on it!

And that's how I became a political activist with him. We put up posters, sold newsletters, and raised funds door-to-door. We debated things, argued a lot: *I mean,* how *could an imperialist war like that have happened?* That was Stieg, a talker, curious about everything, generous, a very moral person. A bit casual for an intellectual, but absolutely irresistible. He fascinated me. There was nothing theoretical about the way he spoke from the heart, from his gut, and yet he was entertaining, too. Politics with him was not a chore or a duty, the way I'd thought it would be, but a real pleasure—which was something of a rare experience in our austere milieu. Stieg and I often thought along the same lines, while most other FNL supporters were Maoists spouting rather unrealistic, authoritarian dogma. Not us.

I found Stieg's ideas so interesting that I began encouraging him to write about them. In Sweden, even small newspapers have a spot in their Arts & Leisure pages for opinion pieces. My father was a journalist and could have helped him, but Stieg, unsure of himself, wouldn't hear of it. I kept pushing him, though, so he finally took the plunge, and when he saw his first published article, he was so thrilled that I think he decided to become a journalist on the spot. He took the entrance exam for a journalism school, failed it (which wasn't surprising, given how young he was), and like most of the other students, could have taken it again, but he refused. His self-confidence was at a low ebb again.

As for me, intrigued at first by the Maoist doctrine, I was going to meetings and even to introductory courses on the subject, which at the time was quite the thing to do. A rational person, I was looking for answers to my questions—but in the wrong places, as it turned out: the Maoist arguments were a bit fuzzy, lightweight, even childish, as if we were going to solve economic problems by simply walking on water! When the Trotskyites showed up and joined forces for a while with the Maoists, they shared the same bank account to raise funds for Vietnam, which I thought was a great idea: at last we were struggling together toward the same goal. Unfortunately, since all revolutionaries want to make their own revolutions, internal power struggles soon broke out. One day we were asked to drum up some money for the Khmer Rouge in Cambodia, and since we had to support their politics, I wanted to know what they were. The answer arrived from on high: "Don't ask questions, do as you're told!" Well, Stieg and I abandoned that fund-raising effort and left the Vietnamese solidarity movement.

I then gravitated toward "the traitors": that's what the Maoists called the Trotskyites, whose system authorized multi-partyism (which I found more democratic), whereas the Maoists were a dictatorship. Stieg decided to stick with the latter, and throughout the year that followed, before we'd moved in together, we fought violently over the best way to bring happiness to the world proletariat. It was awful. And often ended in tears. I thought Stieg was a stupid dreamer with his head in the clouds. At the time, I was living in a student room; I'd been accepted at the Chalmers University of Technology at Gothenburg but decided to register instead at the department of mathematics and economic history at Umeå University, because that way I could stay with Stieg, who had a small studio apartment in Umeå. When we first met, Stieg had been finishing up a two-year program that would allow him to enter the working world but not to attend college. Perhaps he was influenced by my example, who knows, but he then returned to high school for another two years to obtain his baccalaureate degree—and being as stubborn as he was, he got it, which didn't surprise me at all.

He earned his living with odd jobs: delivering papers, working as a locksmith's apprentice, a forester, a dishwasher in a restaurant, and so on. Although we disagreed about how the world works, we knew how to keep our love life separate from our political commitments, and eventually we moved into a large communal apartment with my sister and some friends.

Later on, Stieg in turn joined the Trotskyites. More senior in the movement than he was, I was in charge at the time of a youth group in the high school where he was working toward his diploma. Our roles had been reversed: I was now the teacher, and he the student.

Then the Trotskyist movement asked the students to "proletarianize" themselves by adopting a life of wage labor, and a cell soon sprang up in the local Volvo factory. My working pals were categorical on this point, however: "*We* had no choice, no chance to study. But you do! Continue, absolutely!" And I agreed with them. Ours was the first generation to benefit from government loans for higher education, so why throw it all away? Besides, my background wasn't middle class, my family had been farmers, so I knew perfectly well what the proletariat was—and saw no benefit to society in seeking to rejoin it! City kids kept showing up in bead necklaces and clothes they'd sewn themselves, eager to live communally and go back to the land. We, who actually came from there—we figured they must be off their rockers!

When teaching my classes, I'd use aspects of these young people's lives to get them thinking about things. This was in 1976. My superiors would have liked me just to drill them in theory. I was dismissed from my position, replaced by someone more "red," and I left the Trotskyites. Not Stieg. He stayed in that organization until late in the 1980s, but more for the theory than the practice, as a way to continue the political and intellectual exchanges that so impassioned him. For a long time he also contributed unpaid articles under his own name to *The International*, the official journal of the movement.

In *The Girl Who Played with Fire*, Lisbeth Salander is suspected of murdering the journalist Dag Svensson (whose investigative report on the sex trafficking of Eastern European women was published in the magazine *Millennium*) and his companion Mia Bergman, a criminologist specializing in sexual slavery. Lisbeth discovers she's being sought by the police when she happens to watch part of a television program in which Peter Teleborian, the assistant head physician at St. Stefan's Psychiatric Clinic for Children, outside Uppsala, is pontificating about her case. Lisbeth had been a virtual prisoner in this clinic for more than two years, and she realizes that no newspaper has questioned the fact that doctors are allowed to restrain unruly and difficult patients in a room "free of stimuli" for unconscionable periods of time—a practice she compares to the treatment of political prisoners during the Moscow show trials in the 1930s. Lisbeth knows that "according to the Geneva Conventions, subjecting prisoners to sensory deprivation was classified as inhumane." And this is a topic Stieg and I knew well, because for many years we read everything we could find on it. Stalin treated political opponents as if they were traitors, making them physically disappear—even from photographs, books, and all documentary references—in order to completely rewrite history. The expression "Moscow trial" became part of our private vocabulary.

Using the same words, sharing the same tastes, wanting the same things—that's rather typical of couples who met when they were teenagers and grew into adulthood together.

And yet, it's difficult to explain now how strongly Stieg and I felt, from the first moment we met, that we were made for each other. More than ten years later, he wrote, "I'd given up believing it could happen. I never imagined I'd meet someone like you, who would understand me." For my part, I'd known right away that this man would put the puzzle of my life in order and make me a better person.

But at the same time, finding each other like that put enormous pressure on us. How can anyone calmly accept that his or her life and very *self* should be completely challenged and changed? It was an anguishing feeling, like the realization that the universe is infinite. Sometimes we tried to pull back a little, to get some perspective, but the attraction we felt was too strong. We were afraid, but we were each in thrall to the other.

For thirty-two years, we always had something to say, to tell each other, to explore, to share, to read, to seek, to fight for, and to build . . . together.

And we had wonderful times, too. He was great fun to be with.

He was a loving and demonstrative man. A real teddy bear.

With Stieg, I understood the expression "soul mate."

The Trip to Africa

IN FEBRUARY 1977, when he was twenty-two, one of Stieg's dreams came true: he went to Africa.

To finance his trip, he worked hard for six months at the nearby sawmill in Hörnefors. Why did he go to Africa? He never fully explained that to me, and rightly so: all I knew was that he was leaving on a mission for the Fourth International, the communist organization founded in 1938 in France by Trotsky and his supporters, whom Stalin had driven out of the Soviet Union for their opposition to the Third International. Stieg's assignment was to contact certain groups involved in the civil war then raging in Ethiopia, probably in order to deliver some money and/or documents to them. A risky business. Stieg later told me that just by chance he wound up teaching a female militia unit how to fire mortars—which he'd learned to do during his military service—with weapons smuggled into the hills of Eritrea by the USSR.

Africa fascinated Stieg, and his ambition was to write articles about this continent where so much was happening so quickly. Between his departure in February and his return in July, however, not a single newspaper showed interest in any topic he suggested. Stieg probably seemed too young and inexperienced for the job, but no other journalists, Swedish or otherwise, were on the ground during the Eritrean–Ethiopian War. It was too dangerous.

When he left Umeå, Stieg passed through Stockholm to get his visas, and when I joined him there to say goodbye, he met me at the station, wild with joy.

In the months that followed, his letters arrived at irregular intervals from very different places. He wrote quite guardedly both to me and in the journal he kept on his trip, in which nothing of what he later told me was recorded. Fearing he might be arrested at any moment, he was afraid any important information would fall into the wrong hands, causing serious consequences for him and the people he was meeting.

Stieg caught malaria in Africa and became deathly ill. One day he suddenly went blind: lost in a white fog, he barely managed to return through the streets to his hotel by feeling his way along the sides of buildings. When he reached his room, he passed out, but after someone found him he was rushed to a hospital. Sometime later, he wrote me about his ordeal in a letter that arrived one summer day and scared the wits out of me. It was horrible to read that his kidneys had shut down and that he'd awakened in the hospital to find dried blood from the previous patient on his pillow—only to lose consciousness again.

All in the same letter, I learned that he had almost died, that he realized how important I was to him and how much he loved me, and that he wanted to live with me from now on, as soon as he got home. I'd known that our relationship was deep and strong, but never before had he told me so with such heartfelt sincerity. I cried all through his letter, from fear, relief, and happiness.

He had survived, and we were going to build our life together.

Stockholm

AT UMEÅ University, the various courses I was taking were culturally enriching, but not enough to make me want to take exams and pursue a degree in those fields. So it was time for me to choose a profession. I picked architecture, a discipline that brought together everything I loved in the way of technical skills and creative energy. In 1977 I enrolled in the department of architecture at the Royal Institute of Technology in Stockholm. Stieg arrived a few months later. Housing was already in short supply in the capital, so we stayed in a student room loaned to me by Svante Branden, a psychiatrist friend of Stieg's who was also his neighbor in Umeå.

Svante turns up in *The Girl Who Kicked the Hornet's Nest*, the third volume of the trilogy, when he helps out Lisbeth

Salander by denouncing the fraudulent analysis of Dr. Peter Teleborian and the arbitrary internment to which he had subjected her. That would have been just like Svante, because along with all our other friends, he was against every form of violation of human rights and freedom. When Stieg made him one of the heroes of *The Millennium Trilogy*, it was a way of paying homage to him.

Living at Svante's place all the time was complicated because it was illegal for more than one person to stay there. In those days, young people were allowed to move into buildings slated for demolition and pay a reduced rent for places without any heat or hot water, but such lodgings were really too uncomfortable, so we didn't take much advantage of them. Stieg then managed to find something in a southern suburb of Stockholm. It wasn't until 1979 that I snagged one of the tiny two-room apartments in the Rinkeby district, which are reserved for university students. We lived in that apartment for six years, and we loved the neighborhood so much that when we moved, we found another place there. In the end, we stayed in Rinkeby for twelve years, at a time when few Swedish people lived in an area full of immigrants. Today the population includes more than seventy nationalities, but Rinkeby was already a wonderful melting pot of exotic cultures, which is reflected in the various foreign family names in *The Millennium Trilogy*. I earned my degree in architecture through a project related to the rehabilitation of the district, where most businesses were housed in basements; my proposal envisioned the transformation of the downtown area by creating specific commercial spaces that would favor a more vibrant urban neighborhood atmosphere.

It was hard to find our own apartment in Stockholm, of course, but well worth the trouble, because we adored living there. Our favorite café was run by Greeks, the neighbors on our floor were Finns, those in the apartment below us were Roma, "gypsies," and the tenants on the ground floor were Turks. The husband in the Roma apartment was often in jail, and when he was home, he beat his wife. I remember one time when she managed to escape and come ring our doorbell. Stieg offered her coffee, wiped the blood off her face, and called the police. Calm was restored. Then the Finnish woman next door got up a petition to have her thrown out of the building, so I contacted Social Services (which had a special program for the Roma) to explain that the poor woman was now trapped between the beatings and the threat of eviction. Things settled down again. One evening, when Stieg and I walked into the building, we noticed a strong smell of perfume wafting down the stairs. When we reached our apartment, we saw that the Finnish woman's door was open—and there she was with the Roma, both ladies all dolled up for a night on the town! That was Rinkeby for you.

I can honestly say that I was never afraid to come home in the evening, even after Stieg began to focus on right-wing extremists and we started receiving threats. We had the whole world at our doorstep, we didn't need to travel abroad. In fact, when we moved into Stockholm proper in

1991, it was a real culture shock to find ourselves in a city that was so ethnically homogeneous.

◻

IN ADDITION to politics, Stieg and I had long shared a common passion for science fiction. Our favorite authors were Robert Heinlein and Samuel R. Delany, and I had translated into Swedish Philip K. Dick's *The Man in the High Castle*, which describes what the world would be like if the Nazis had won World War II. As soon as we'd moved to Stockholm, we'd joined the largest Swedish science fiction fan club, the SFSF (Skandinavisk Förening för Science Fiction), a friendly and varied collection of likeable weirdos, all of them crazy about SF. We fit right in. For two years, we were the editors in chief of *Fanac*, the SFSF newsletter, and from time to time we managed the association's science fiction bookstore on Kungsholmen, a large island to the northwest of Södermalm in Lake Mälaren and part of the city of Stockholm. As business ventures go, the bookstore and newsletter were duds, but that wasn't important, because *fandom is a way of life*. We were dreamers, fascinated by the alternative universes we found in that literature. Especially when they became real on the Internet. Published in 1992, Neal Stephenson's *Snow Crash* is a good example of the cyberpunk milieu reflected in the cybernetic world of the hacker republic in which Lisbeth Salander is a model citizen.

In science fiction, cyborgs—half human, half machine—can plug directly into computers to join up with the cyberworld. Lisbeth Salander plugs herself into the Internet, and her extraordinary skills are quite close to those of a cyborg. *The Millennium Trilogy* could have made a good SF saga, too.

At that time Stieg had a job in the postal service, and I had my state scholarship. Our two incomes allowed us to live, but nothing more, especially since Stieg, unlike me, was a spendthrift. For example, even when we were practically broke, he always had breakfast at the café although it was rather expensive. I could point this out to him as often as I liked, but that's how it was, he didn't want to change. I was from a family of country people who had some land and a farm, true, but no money to spare. Stieg's parents owned nothing and rented their apartment, but their furniture was actually more expensive than my family's. Since they worked in a clothing store, they had lots of clothes at home and Vivianne, Stieg's mother, would often give me some.

◙

A FEW months after we moved to Stockholm, my father died. He was barely forty-six, an alcoholic, and he had started taking medications even though he was drinking, which is dangerous.

Two years earlier, he'd fallen so deeply into debt that almost everything except the family farm had been sold at auction. We'd also managed to save that little cabin and its forest in Önnesmark, sixty miles from Umeå, which Stieg and I used to go take care of with my brother and sister every so often. When he'd drawn up the inventory, the bailiff had shown an interest in the property, but my father—or perhaps Vivianne, Stieg's mother—had come up with a way to save it. Stieg and I were clearly a couple, and our families knew each other, so they worked together on this. My father signed a lifetime lease on the property for Stieg's parents, which meant the cabin and forest could no longer be sold. Erland and Vivianne were very happy to spend all their summers there, and planted potatoes and strawberries on the property.

After the auction, my father's debts were discharged and there was even a little money left over. After his death, however, we discovered that he had spent everything and gone into debt again, so we had to sell the farmhouse and its contents. At that time, my brother and sister and I were still students and had left all our belongings in the house. Everything vanished: our books, schoolwork, photos—everything. Two hundred years of family memories. My grandmother was grief-stricken at losing her only son. As for everything else . . . she behaved once again with great dignity. Accepting her fate, she moved into the village retirement home where she lived for another fifteen years without complaint.

Stieg was deeply distressed by what had happened. My father had been very fond of him, and was the only person with whom Stieg could talk about journalism. As for me, I was in a state of collapse. Stieg wrapped a protective cocoon around me. He supported me so much that I can truly say he carried me through that awful period of my life.

The TT Agency

IN 1979, Stieg left the postal service and joined TT (Tidningarnas Telegrambyrå), the big Swedish news agency, our equivalent of the Associated Press. He stayed there for twenty years. Starting out in the editorial department, he manned the phone as a kind of editorial secretary, receiving news items and articles from the reporters in all of the news services and correcting the copy before it went off to various papers. Then he became an illustrator in the TT Images and Features department, where he could also write about many subjects that interested him: Darwin, Robin Hood, World War II—you name it. Not to mention crime novels, which were also one of his specialties. In particular those written by women, whose style he found in general much better than that of most men. A typical autodidact, Stieg had a vast fount of eclectic knowledge at his fingertips, and our home was always cluttered with books on all sorts of subjects: science fiction, politics, espionage, counterespionage, military strategy, feminism, computer science, and so on. To get them as cheaply as possible, we bought them in the original version, usually in English. Most of his colleagues saw Stieg as a pleasant person, intelligent, but difficult to get a handle on, especially since he tended to keep his private life to himself. Around the mid-1980s, when militants on the extreme right began robbing banks to finance their activities, breaking into military installations to steal weapons, and killing people for racist or political reasons, the Legal Affairs and News in Brief department within the agency began consulting Stieg. More often than not, he would know the past political affiliations of the suspects, their accomplices, and even the milieus they frequented! Working his way through a mass of often contradictory data, Stieg would swiftly figure out what was really going on. In 1999, for example, at the time of the Oklahoma City bombing, which killed 168 people and wounded 680, Stieg understood from the beginning—unlike all the media—that the culprit was most likely an American militia member inspired by the far-right rhetoric of William Pierce's *Turner Diaries*.

From the 1990s on, TT topped the list of the news media best informed about such subjects. The number one expert in this domain was right there at TT, and yet, even with the support of the other journalists, Stieg was never transferred to a job at any of the regular desks. Reason given: "Stieg Larsson cannot write." What do the millions of readers of *The Millennium Trilogy* think about that?

▣

IN THE mid-1990s, the media struggled through a severe economic crisis. Ad pages fell sharply, lots of journalists were laid off, and various newspapers folded. Although TT did not escape this storm battering the print press, the small Images and Features department kept doing well, selling photos and articles—in fact, against all expectations, it even made a profit. In spite of this, when the agency began downsizing across the board to increase efficiency, Stieg's entire department was eliminated. This was the opportune moment to move Stieg to the Legal Affairs and News in Brief section, because he had recently proved, once again, that it was the right place for him.

In the aftermath of a bank robbery in 1999, two police officers had been killed execution-style in Malexander, a village a hundred miles from Stockholm. The circumstances surrounding these murders alerted Stieg to a connection with the extreme right, which later proved correct, but the manager in charge of staff layoffs refused to transfer Stieg, falling back on the same old argument: "Stieg Larsson cannot write!" Stieg and I talked and argued a great deal about what he should do. I thought it was high time for him to devote more than weekends and evenings late into the night to his passion for investigative journalism. True, we hadn't any savings and earned only enough to pay our basic expenses, and I couldn't remember buying any clothes that weren't on sale or shopping anywhere but in a discount store. Still, even though it was financially risky, the moment had come for him to strike out on his own.

In the end, realizing that he would never get ahead at TT, Stieg chose to take the severance package and was let go in 1999.

◻

SO HE walked away from twenty years of work at TT and never went back. Later on, when he had appointments with journalists still at the agency, he met them in a café. Stieg never forgot or forgave what he and other perfectly competent journalists had gone through during the almost completely irrational dismemberment of Sweden's greatest news agency.

From that moment on, he devoted himself entirely to the Swedish Expo Foundation, which he had cofounded earlier, in 1995, and to its quarterly magazine, *Expo*.

Expo

DEEPLY IMPRESSED as a child by his grandfather's anti-Nazi political engagement, Stieg wanted to write for *Searchlight*, a British antifascist magazine he admired, and back in 1982 he had gone to London to meet Graeme Atkinson, the editor. They rendezvoused at a café, and since they were complete strangers, they began with a cautious "security check" by submitting each other to an in-depth interrogation about fascism. It's a good thing they shared the same sense of humor! That turned out to be the decisive factor in establishing trust between them. In 1983 Stieg started writing for the magazine under a pseudonym, like all the other contributors. *Searchlight* was the sole exception here, however, because Stieg signed his own name, for example, to the section on Scandinavia that appears in *Les Extrémismes en Europe*, by the French political economist Jean-Yves Camus—as he did with every other article, report, and book he ever wrote.

After Stieg's death and the success of *The Millennium Trilogy*, a British publisher wanted to bring out a collection of all his articles written for *Searchlight*, but was rebuffed by the magazine. He even came to Stockholm to ask me to put pressure on the magazine's editor to change his mind, and the man was so insistent that I showed him the letter I'd received from *Searchlight* saying that *not one comma* of those articles would be handed over to the "Stieg industry." I was truly moved by the editorial staff's respect for their collaborator of over twenty years.

After a wave of racist violence in the 1980s, the extreme right became increasingly active in Sweden in the early 1990s. Stieg and I felt it was vital to have a magazine like *Searchlight* in our country, but British culture is quite different from ours, and we didn't want simply to create a copycat. Along with a group of like-minded people, we spent over two years in endless theoretical discussions debating the kinds of things our magazine should publish.

Founded in 1985 and inspired by the antiracist French NGO SOS Racisme and its yellow hand logo (bearing the slogan *Touche pas à mon pote*, which means "Hands off my pal!"), the organization Stop Racism decided in 1995 to enrich its newsletter with a supplement carrying in-depth articles on racist and extreme-right groups. When we joined forces with them, things took off. We suddenly had more people, subsidies, and a concept—but no name. The magazine was christened *Expo*. After three issues, the staff decided that the magazine would work better on its own, without ties to an association. Stieg and I were really pleased to have young people join in, and we tried to give them as much autonomy as possible. They worked in a basement on a street where Lisbeth Salander lives for a while, in a space like the tiny, stuffy cellar where *Millennium* was born. At one point *Expo* had its headquarters in an apartment over the Kaffebar—a coffee bar on Hornsgatan—where Mikael Blomkvist often meets with people. (In Swedish, *gatan* means "street," and Hornsgatan is one of the main streets of the Södermalm district in Stockholm.) The *Expo* staff was constantly changing locations to escape harassment by neo-Nazi groups, for there was no denying the fact that *Expo*'s debut had provoked serious opposition. That April, a small extremist group began issuing threats and vandalizing the premises of all of the parties in Parliament that supported *Expo* through their Youth Activities sections. Press and book outlets, like the large newsstand on Odengatan, saw their display windows smashed, while the printing house was tagged with swastikas and the warning "Don't print *Expo*." The political parties refused to be intimidated, but the printing house tossed in the towel.

And that led to a sensational development in June 1996: the largest national evening papers, *Aftonbladet* and *Expressen*, decided that they would print the current issue of *Expo* with no strings attached, distributing it as a special supplement to their daily papers. Both editors in chief,

Torbjörn Larsson and Christina Jutterström, wrote a joint editorial explaining that they wished through their action to defend freedom of speech. Stieg was beside himself with delight. Thanks to this decisive intervention, *Expo* managed to keep going on its own until 1997, but donations and subscription fees barely covered the rent and printing costs. When the economic crisis arrived, *Expo* began to falter. In an attempt to save it, we contacted the National Council of Culture, but the grant we received was so small that the editorial staff gave up in exhaustion. (Naturally, everyone had been working full tilt on the magazine in whatever spare time we had—in the evening, during the night, on weekends.) So *Expo* ceased regular publication, continuing to appear only as a supplement in various publications such as *Monitor*, a Norwegian antiracist magazine, in 1998, and later in Kurt Baksi's magazine *Svartvitt* (*Black/White*). In this way *Expo* managed to stay alive thanks to a kind of artificial respiration, but it would be five years before it could appear regularly again as an independent publication.

For Stieg and me, the 1990s were a grueling period during which he worked like a man possessed. What with his job at TT, his work for *Searchlight*, *Expo*, and the books he was writing or on which he was collaborating, there really wasn't any time left for me. I felt very lonely, especially after the financial crash in 1993 cost me my job as an architect in a large construction company, where I'd been thrilled to be working on exciting projects such as the Soder Crescent, an elegant residential complex designed by the Catalan postmodernist architect Ricardo Bofill.

Stieg and I were on such different schedules that some-times we had to make an appointment even to see each other! Snatching some time between TT and *Expo*, he'd meet me at the Kafé Anna (which turns up in the trilogy, of course) to have a caffe latte together.

I left Stieg twice during those years, even if it was only for a few weeks. The first time, I went to live in an apart-ment lent to me by a friend, and the next time I stayed with my friend Eleanor. Each time, Stieg was in despair, and even today I feel awful for having put him through that pain—a man who had suffered from such a profound sense of abandonment as a child when his grandfather died. I should have found another way to make him understand that I needed him, especially since these wrenching sepa-rations managed to improve our lives, in spite of his efforts, for only a few months before he would quickly be over-whelmed with work again.

1999 was the year of greatest change and greatest risk. Stieg decided to leave TT, as I've already noted, and ex-treme-right violence in Sweden increased dramatically. Once more, Stieg paid homage in *The Millennium Trilogy* to an "ordinary hero" through his inclusion of Hallvigs Reklam AB in Morgongåva (in Uppsala County, just north of Stockholm), the publishing company that took over from the one that stopped printing *Expo* after receiving se-rious threats. The owner of Hallvigs, Jan Köbin, made a great impression on Stieg because he didn't hesitate to use his own car to ensure that every last issue of *Expo* was de-livered on time, and I was pleased when he was named

Sweden's Businessman of the Year in 2007. In the first book of the trilogy, Mikael Blomkvist entrusts to Jan Köbin the printing of his book on the Wennerström affair and the special issue of *Millennium* that will reveal this scandal. In the second volume, Blomkvist again puts his faith in the printer who offers "the best price and service in the industry," giving him Dag's book on the sex-trafficking networks in Eastern Europe. And in the third volume, it's Köbin again who prints the book exposing the Section, the secret organization of spies created during the Cold War.

Expo continued to survive as best it could thanks to the very things that power the magazine *Millennium*: the enthusiasm of all sorts of people for a common project in which they strongly believe. In a scene in *The Girl Who Played with Fire*, Erika Berger prepares coffee in the magazine office's kitchenette, and Stieg has her smiling at the sight of so many mismatched mugs all bearing the logos of different political parties. It was an affectionate wink at *Expo*, where the cups were as varied as the opinions of the journalists, who were allowed to support any party they wanted—but not as active members. This strict rule guaranteed the independence of the magazine, so that it would never be caught up in political rivalries.

After years of dependence on other publications, *Expo* officially resurfaced in 2003 thanks to grants we obtained to fund two projects: school programs fostering the culture of democracy among young people, and the production of RAXEN reports for the EUMC. These reports by the Racism and Xenophobia European Network for the

EU's Monitoring Centre examined the incidence of racial discrimination and racist crimes in various sectors such as housing and employment.

So a few salaries were assured, one of them Stieg's. We had a new team, still as young as before but more professional, most of whom had journalistic experience. I dealt only with those RAXEN reports, which I fact-checked, completed, or translated into English. It was a rather "dry" job, sort of like editing, but a necessary one, since the reports were our main source of income. I remember our New Year's Eve in 2002, when we worked through the night on a report that absolutely had to be delivered by January 1. A few of our fellow workers peeled off at some point to go celebrate, but we "old folks" stayed on to meet our deadline.

Throughout our years of political struggle against the extreme right, Stieg wrote constantly, hoping to sound the alarm about nationalist political parties like the Sweden Democrats. He tried to show that they weren't simply a gang of madmen plotting to infiltrate Swedish society (as one conspiracy theory had it), but a real political movement that had to be combated through political means. Given what is happening in Sweden today, with the SD now represented in the Swedish Parliament, it seems clear that Stieg's nightmare has come true. . . .

Threats

WHEN HE began writing for *Searchlight* and its antifascist agenda, Stieg, too, became a hated enemy of the far right. In the spring of 1991, he published *Extremhögern* (*Right-Wing Extremism*) with Anna-Lena Lodenius. The book provided an overview of all the groups and parties at that end of the political spectrum, covering the origins of their movements, their use of violence, and their current affiliated organizations in Europe, Scandinavia, and the United States. It was the first comprehensive work ever published on the subject. One of the groups mentioned in the book, VAM (Vitt Ariskt Motstand, for White Aryan Resistance), published a magazine called *Storm* that was steeped in racial violence dressed up in a romantic aura. Seven of its members had amassed a total of twenty convictions among them for crimes such as armed robbery, stealing weapons from military depots, and homicide, so when we learned the following year that *Storm* knew both our address and that of Anna-Lena, we were worried: having your name on neo-Nazi hit lists can be very dangerous.

While we were trying to figure out how to react and protect ourselves, my sister's companion at the time told us, "You're part of the family. I'll go see my uncle, an Italian; he's connected, he'll come up with a definitive solution for you." At first we were delighted with the offer, especially with its suggestion of an "extended family." Then we had second thoughts. We knew perfectly well there'd be no question of money changing hands, and that one day we'd be expected to repay a debt of honor. *But what form would it take?* Besides, finding criminals was the job of the police. So we declined the invitation, explaining that we preferred to let the law take its course. I admit, though, that I thought about that idea for some time. In 1993, *Storm* published photos of Stieg and Anna-Lena along with their social security and phone numbers, plus their personal and business addresses. Referring to Stieg, the accompanying text concluded: "Never forget his words, his face, and his address. Should he be allowed to continue his work—or should he be dealt with?"

In those days, anyone could obtain pictures of any Swedish citizen by going to the passport service of the Swedish police. In *The Girl with the Dragon Tattoo*, Lisbeth Salander explains how simple it is to do so: "If the person is in a database, which is absolutely the case for everyone, the target swiftly winds up in the spider's web." In the next book, *The Girl Who Played with Fire*, Lisbeth even hesitates to move to another apartment because that would mean a new address and would make her "someone concretely present in all sorts of computer files." Stieg knew everything there was to know about tracking people, all the methods used by journalists, by the police, by men hunting for the wives who'd left them after conjugal violence, and as it happens—by extremists and criminal gangs. Because of the threats from *Storm*, the magazine was prosecuted and convicted. But that took time. . . .

In the 1990s, more than a dozen people were murdered in Sweden for political reasons by individuals involved with neo-Nazi groups. Säpo—the Security Service, an arm of the Swedish National Police—estimates that during 1998 alone, there were more than two thousand unprovoked racist attacks, more than half of which can be directly linked to neo-Nazi militants in White Power groups. And some of these extremists had managed to obtain our phone number, because although only my name appeared on our apartment door, and the telephone was listed under my name alone, we were receiving anonymous calls. Our apartment was already secured by an alarm system and a digicode keypad, but I had a new metal security door installed as well. After Mikael Blomkvist enters Lisbeth Salander's swank new apartment at 9 Fiskargatan in the Mosebacke area of Södermalm, he stares in frustration at the alarm keypad by the front door. He knows that if he doesn't tap in the correct four-digit code within thirty seconds, the alarm will go off and a bunch of beefy guys from a security company will arrive in no time. Stieg and I went through that experience many times when we'd come home exhausted only to find ourselves standing at our front door, powerless to stop the "screamer"—our pet name for the alarm.

Now and then Stieg would receive bullets in the mail, and once someone was waiting for him outside the entrance to the TT building. Warned in time, Stieg slipped out a back door. Our answering machine was set permanently on "Record" to keep evidence of the threats we received, and they were always in the same vein: "Piece of shit, you Jew-fucker. . . . Traitor, we'll tear you apart . . . and we know where you live. . . ."

Swedish neo-Nazis have their own information network: the Anti-AFA (Anti-Anti-Fascist Action). In 1994, after the complaint lodged against *Storm*, the police seized a list of over two hundred antiracist activists. A few years later, extremists targeted Peter Karlsson and Katarina Larsson, two journalists at *Aftonbladet*—one of Sweden's largest evening papers—who had once worked with us at *Expo*. At the time, they were investigating, among other things, the flourishing White Power music industry, which finances extremist groups throughout the world, and their efforts would later help lead to the bankruptcy of the racist Nordland music label in Sweden. Although they were allowed to officially conceal their identities in public records, their names, addresses, and detailed personal information about them were posted on the Internet in March 1999. Not long afterward, *Aftonbladet* published their reporters' findings in an article revealing the names of neo-Nazis who had received training in weapons and explosives during their military service. Three months later, on June 28, Peter Karlsson and his eight-year-old son were the victims of a car bomb. When the little boy opened the car door, he was thrown back from the blast and only slightly injured, but his father sustained a serious spinal injury and remains severely handicapped.

On September 16 of that same year, trade unionist Björn Söderberg revealed that a neo-Nazi had been elected to the board of his local employees' union. That same day and throughout the month of September, photos of more than twenty-five antiextremist activists, including that of Björn Söderberg, were requested from the passport services by the neo-Nazi newspaper *Info 14*. On October 12, Björn Söderberg was murdered, shot multiple times at his home in a Stockholm suburb. Among the possessions of one of the men implicated in his assassination, the police later found a list of more than a thousand names!

Events like these back up the threats directed at the magazine *Millennium* and underline the failings of the security measures provided by the state for any of the novel's public citizens put at risk, failings that lead to the murders of Dag Svensson and Mia Bergman in *The Girl Who Played with Fire*. In fact, everything of this nature described in *The Millennium Trilogy* has happened at one time or another to a Swedish citizen, journalist, politician, public prosecutor, unionist, or policeman. *Nothing was made up.*

The culprits were quickly found and arrested on October 14, 1999. Shortly afterward, Stieg called one afternoon to tell me Peter Karlsson had just warned him that our passport photos, along with Söderberg's, had been found among the evidence in the case, and that some of the suspects were still at large. Before hanging up, Stieg told me, "You mustn't go home." When the last member of the group was arrested on November 29, my friend Eleanor told me, relieved, "Now we can finally go out safely in public and stuff ourselves in a restaurant!"

Throughout that period, Stieg and I worried constantly about each other. Even before that, in a café I had always sat between him and the door as a kind of protective screen, but now we weren't allowing ourselves to be seen together at all. My colleagues at work didn't know the name of the man I lived with; I was always evasive, simply saying, "a journalist." I never invited my coworkers home, only to public places. As for Stieg, without saying anything about it, he had set up a security network around me. This meant that if the police got a call reporting an incident on our street, they were authorized to send all available vehicles. I realized this the day there was a minor car accident outside our apartment and I heard so many sirens arrive that I went out on the balcony, saw only a fender bender, and thought, You'd think the cops had nothing better to do!

There wasn't anything brave about living that way. We just did. We'd both chosen that. But it definitely had an effect on our lives. It was why—among other things—we'd never gotten married or had children.

It really was safer for Stieg to remain "single" in all official documents. True, his address was relatively easy to find, as I've explained, but since mine was the only name on our door and on all our bills, tracking down his exact whereabouts was more difficult.

In 1983, we had decided to get married. We bought rings in a store on Regeringsgatan—"Government Street"—and had them engraved with "Stieg and Eva." We made an appointment with the minister of the parish of Spånga in northwest Stockholm to find out how long the necessary formalities would take, only to discover that getting married was more complicated and time-consuming than we'd thought. Once again, our professional obligations got in the way of our private lives, and neither one of us took the time to compile the required administrative dossier.

Then the United States invaded what we thought of as "our island," Grenada. And we worked night and day to find out what had really happened there, so getting married was no longer our top priority. Besides, Stieg had just begun writing for *Searchlight* and started drawing too much interest from the extreme right to take any risks. Even though we weren't married yet, we wore our rings; Stieg finally had to take his off when he gained weight in 1990, but it's on his hand in many of my photographs from those days. As for me, I now wear Stieg's ring as well as my own.

Erland, Stieg's father, urged us several times to get married, especially at the end of the 1980s, when there was talk of eliminating the reversion of pensions on the death of a spouse if the marriage had not taken place before a certain date. Like many couples of our generation, however, we did not follow through. And with good reason, since we had to consider the very real problem of our personal safety.

I also think that our respective childhoods did not condition us to have a family. When I was a little girl, I believed my mother had abandoned me. The reality was much more complex than that, of course, but that event certainly contributed to my fear of having a child. We thought about having one, naturally, but—and I mean this without any "irony"—there was always something more urgent to take care of: we wanted our financial situation to be more stable, more promising, more *secure*—before taking such an important step. . . . And time passed. . . .

A few months before his death, Stieg talked again about getting married. Especially since we already had our rings! With the *Millennium* books about to be published, we knew that our personal finances would improve, and since Stieg had decided to work only part-time at *Expo*, he would be less at risk from right-wing retaliation.

This time, it was death that overshadowed our private lives.

Millennium

STIEG DID not sit down one day at his computer and announce, "I'm going to write a crime novel!" In a way, he never even formally began to write one at all, because he never drew up an outline for the first book, or the next two, still less for the seven he intended should follow.

Stieg wrote sequences that were often unrelated to the others. Then he would "stitch" them together, following the thread of the story and his inclination.

In 2002, during a week's island vacation, I could see he was a bit bored. I was working on my book about the Swedish architect Per Olof Hallman (1869–1941, a professional town planner), but Stieg was at loose ends, going around in circles.

So I asked him, "Haven't you got some writing to work on?"

"No, but I was just thinking about that piece I wrote in 1997, the one about the old man who receives a flower in the mail every year at Christmas. Remember?"

"Of course!"

"I've been wondering for a long time what that was really all about."

Stieg got right to it and we spent the rest of the week working outdoors on our computers, with the sea before our eyes and grass beneath our feet. Happy.

So my book and the trilogy took shape at the same time.

Contrary to what most people think, Stieg wasn't a computer whiz, and he even used a typewriter for most of his writing life. We switched to computers only in the early 1990s, after I'd worked for a business that used them. Even at *Expo*, we had to call in a team of experts to protect our computers from hacking, because none of us was up to the job. And Stieg wasn't a math nut, either, in spite of Lisbeth Salander's fascination when she discovers Fermat's Last Theorem in *The Girl Who Played with Fire*, a fascination Stieg describes over several pages here and there in the trilogy until Lisbeth loses interest in that mystery in the third volume. Actually, Stieg was always terrible at math, which almost cost him his baccalaureate exam, but the theorem typified the kind of knowledge we both loved: a heterogeneous, eccentric store of learning that wasn't necessarily useful in life, yet delighted us. Sometimes reading a single sentence on an unfamiliar subject would inspire us to delve deeply into its mysteries. Stieg was like a sponge, absorbing everything, and without ever taking notes! For example, to come up with the clothes his characters wore, which were always described in great detail, he never consulted any catalogues or peered into any shopwindows. All he did was study fashion in the street. And he loved that. Stieg had a very personal way of dressing. Unlike most people in his milieu, who generally favored sporty casual dress for every occasion, he wore tweed jackets, elegant but inexpensive, and he adapted his style to the people and situations he encountered. He had class, without ever coming across as a dandy or a snob.

In two years, he wrote two thousand pages of the trilogy. Whether it was for *Searchlight*, TT, *Expo*, or the trilogy, he always tackled his writing with the same energy. During the first year he worked evenings and weekends, going to bed late but no more so than usual. This sometimes made life hard for me, but our saving grace was that we laughed a lot. He'd take a break, go smoke a cigarette out on the balcony, then get back to work with renewed concentration. During that last year, he was also writing during the day and in the *Expo* office instead of dealing with his magazine work. That was the year he worked so hard he slept barely five or six hours a night. Whenever I would reread the texts that came toward the end of the trilogy, I'd notice that he'd written them at around three or four in the morning. I believe *The Millennium Trilogy* had become a refuge for him.

Stieg was an artist, so he did not always have his feet planted firmly on the ground. At home, I was there, "the artist's wife," to take care of daily life, but at *Expo* things were a royal mess. Stieg was a good editor in chief for the magazine but a poor director for the foundation. Not only was he disorganized and completely on his own, but there was never enough money, either. He had no idea how to control or keep track of ongoing projects and was constantly exhausted from having to solve problems in haste and under pressure. After his death, I found a letter addressed to the foundation's sponsors asking them once again for financial aid; dated November 7, it had never been sent. Stieg died on November 9. In the end, all the gratitude and praise heaped on *Expo* for its wonderful work were just words. Stieg had to fight to find a way to make it to the end of every month, and the worst part of it was—he was losing heart. He'd left TT, his severance pay was gone, and his hopes for *Expo* were foundering. Everything he'd believed in was going up in smoke. So he wrote and wrote. It was like therapy. He was describing Sweden the way it was and the way he saw his country: the scandals, the oppression of women, the friends he cherished and wished to honor, Grenada—that island so dear to us. . . . He thought out every little detail because he kept everything in his prodigious memory . . . and in his computer.

Without Stieg's battles and crusades, *The Millennium Trilogy* would never have seen the light of day. His struggle is the heart, brain, and brawn of that saga.

Stieg's Journalistic Credo

STIEG CAMPAIGNED for many years to have the Swedish Constitution hold the Internet to the same level of accountability demanded of all other media, namely, the obligation to have a legally responsible publisher. He got nowhere. The result is that even today, racist and fascist websites that incite hatred and threaten innocent people are still beyond the reach of the law.

In June 2004, Stieg raised this question at a conference in Paris presented by the OSCE (Organization for Security and Co-operation in Europe), an ad hoc organization under the United Nations Charter and the world's largest security-oriented intergovernmental body. The OSCE, which comprises fifty-six states in Europe,

Central Asia, and North America, describes itself as "a forum for political negotiations and decision-making in the fields of early warning, conflict prevention, crisis management and post-conflict rehabilitation." During this conference, Stieg spoke out against the danger of leaving the Internet beyond the reach of all legislation. "For racist groups," he said, "cyberspace is a dream. It's no accident that their first priority is to set up a website." But he also warned against considering the law as the sole effective remedy: "In my opinion, legislation alone cannot defeat the challenge posed by hate propaganda on the Internet. In fact I appeal to you: do not put too much trust in legislation."

Stieg felt that without the democratic activism of politicians and citizens (whose ranks include journalists), legislation would never get at the root of the problem, and he was very worried that if nothing was done, the situation was doomed to deteriorate even further.

The Millennium Trilogy accuses the media of gradually abdicating their responsibilities toward society throughout the 1980s and 1990s. Investigative journalists had turned away from social problems, and financial reporters treated CEOs like rock stars, allowing them to quietly enrich themselves through dummy corporations, hefty bonuses, and cartels. That fluid border between businesses and the print media also led many journalists to become public relations directors for big companies. At the beginning of the trilogy, in *The Girl with the Dragon Tattoo*, Mikael Blomkvist describes, in his portrait of William Borg, everything Stieg criticized on that score: Borg had left journalism, "and now he worked in P.R. as a consultant—for a considerably higher salary—at a firm." Stieg never sold himself for money or to further his career.

⊡

STIEG PUT his entire code of journalistic ethics into *The Millennium Trilogy*. And he showed his respect for the reader. "It doesn't matter how many advertisers we have," Mikael tells Henrik Vanger, "if no one wants to buy the magazine." Stieg adamantly championed what every newspaper and magazine owes its readers: the search for the truth. But since he also thought a publication should not sacrifice everything to its readers, he objected to putting rape victims through more suffering by splashing their private lives all over magazines. In the trilogy, he strongly and sarcastically condemns the ever more offensive tactics of this kind, such as the newspaper headlines calling Lisbeth and her friends a "lesbian Satanist gang." And when Mikael Blomkvist solves the mystery of Harriet Vanger's disappearance, he faces a huge problem of conscience. Should he be a good reporter and tell the entire story—at the risk of exposing Harriet to public scrutiny? Or should he keep quiet, thus concealing the truth, despite the financial windfall such a scoop would mean to *Millennium*?

After a long and painful inner struggle, Mikael's conscience wins out over his ego as a reporter: he will not publish the story. This passage was of great importance to Stieg, because he sincerely wanted to send a message, but when I first read the text I disagreed with what he'd written. In that first version, when Mikael finds Harriet out in Australia, she exclaims almost in terror, "So now that you know I'm alive—what are you going to do? Are you going to rape me too?" I felt that readers would take those last words too literally and think Harriet was completely paranoid. Since Stieg was convinced I was wrong, we had argument after argument about this. In the end, he never said, "Okay, I'll change it." He never said anything. But he took out that sentence.

IN THE opening of the first book, after being accused of not verifying the evidence he uses for an exposé of the industrialist Hans-Erik Wennerström, Mikael Blomkvist quits his job as the publisher of *Millennium* because he's afraid that otherwise, readers will lose confidence in the magazine. Later, before he makes public the valid proof that has been gathered by Dag Svensson, he checks all this information with obsessive care. I know that behavior well from having watched Stieg at work, and he really did feel that sources were sacred—which is why Mikael erases from his computer all the files revealing any sources before the police arrive, after Dag and Mia have been murdered. And it makes clearer today why, after Stieg's death, no one in his personal circle, myself included, wanted to say anything about the computer he was using. Besides the fourth *Millennium* novel in progress, it contained the names and contact information of his informants on the far right. And on this point, the Swedish constitution is clear: sources must be protected!

Feminism

THE MILLENNIUM Trilogy is a catalogue of all forms of violence and discrimination endured by women.

When he was a teenager in Umeå, Stieg was devastated by a dramatic incident that marked him for life. One weekend, he witnessed the gang rape of a girl at a campground. Some of the rapists were friends of his, and he refused to have anything to do with them afterward. From that moment on, he blamed himself for not having intervened. A while after that horrible episode, he ran into the girl in town and tried to apologize. Refusing to hear him out, she drew back from him with an accusation he never forgot: "Get away from me! You're one of them!"

Should this experience be seen as the source of his feminism? It most certainly contributed to it. While he was writing the trilogy, Stieg's working title for all three books was *The Men Who Hate Women*. This title was retained only for the first volume of the Swedish edition, and even then, only because he strongly insisted on it. And the word "hate" in the title was replaced by "don't love" in the French edition.

WHEN HE was young, Stieg had played drums with a pal who'd introduced him to jazz, but it was rock he loved best, especially feminine rock like Shakespears Sister, Annie Lennox in the Eurythmics, and Tina Turner. And Lisbeth just happens to have close ties to the girls in a rock band called Evil Fingers. My own tastes are a little broader, from opera through rock and mainstream to pop. At home, Stieg and I listened to different music, but not all that much of the time, actually.

We divided up the housekeeping according to our different inclinations: he liked to do housework, I preferred cooking. Since we both hated doing laundry with a passion, we took turns at that.

When I'd met Stieg in 1972, he was already a staunch feminist who preferred the company of women and liked working with them more than with men. What's more, they generally liked him back: he used to say that when he was a child living with his grandparents, his best friend was—a little girl! He found women more creative and less ambitious, less conniving than men. Wherever he worked, Stieg treated men and women the same way, held them to the same standards, and didn't mind one bit taking orders from women. If he encountered macho careerists who tried to block the advancement of "Stieg's women," he either obliged them to change their attitude or eliminated them from his private life. In *The Girl Who Kicked the Hornet's Nest*, when Erika Berger becomes editor in chief at *SMP* (*Svenska Morgon-Posten*, what Mikael Blomkvist calls "Sweden's most turgid old-boy newspaper"), Stieg gives a clear idea of the kind of hazing and dirty tricks a competent woman must face in a man's world. "An editorial meeting at two o'clock was suddenly moved to one-thirty without her being told, and most of the decisions were already made by the time she arrived." Headlines Erika chooses are replaced and the articles she rejects wind up on page one.

Stieg's obvious fondness for women never really bothered me; neither one of us was jealous, as it happened, but to tell the truth, we did keep an eye on each other!

WOMEN COULDN'T help but play an important role in *The Millennium Trilogy*. Of all different ages and professions, with varying personalities, they have this in common: they are stubborn, like Stieg, and even pigheaded in what they do. Like him, they give as good as they get—and they get their revenge. Stieg saw no excuse for male violence and has Lisbeth say so in no uncertain terms. Martin Vanger was raped by his father, true, but he had "exactly the same opportunity as anyone else to strike back. He killed and he raped because he liked doing it." Later on Lisbeth adds: "I just think that it's pathetic that creeps always have to have someone else to blame."

The murders of three women in particular had a direct influence on *The Millennium Trilogy*. In 2003, after the almost simultaneous killings of Melissa Nordell and Fadime Sahindal, Stieg worked with Cecilia Englund at *Expo* on an anthology entitled *Debatten om heders mord: feminism eller rasism* (*The Debate on Honor Killings: Feminism or Racism?*). Nordell was murdered by her boyfriend, and her body was found in the water near the wharf in Björkvik, a small community on the Stockholm County island of Ingarö. Sahindal was shot in the head by her father because she refused to be forced into marriage. In Sweden, Nordell's death was seen as an ordinary murder, while Sahindal's was considered an ethnic murder, an honor crime, an incident unrelated to "Swedish culture." Stieg called the victims "sisters in death" because he saw them as victims of the same patriarchal oppression. The cultural differences evoked to differentiate between the two killings simply fed racist propaganda and fueled endless academic research. Meanwhile, women kept dying at the hands of men.

In the book on honor crimes, Stieg wrote: "The cultural and anthropological models used to explain these tragedies speak to the form of oppression involved but do not explain it. And so in India, women are set on fire; they are murdered in the name of honor in Sicily; they are beaten up on Saturday night in Sweden. . . . Yet *culture* does not explain why women all over the world are murdered, mutilated, 'circumcised,' mistreated, and forced to submit to ritual behaviors by men. Neither does it explain why men in our patriarchal societies oppress women." And he adds, "*Systematic violence* against women—because this violence is indeed systematic—would be the description used if such violence were directed against union members, Jews, or handicapped persons." Stieg was quite gratified when the other eight contributors to the anthology, six of them women, wholeheartedly agreed with him.

The third murder was that of Catrine Da Costa, parts of whose dismembered body were found in two plastic bags. Stieg had read a fascinating book about that crime. The author, Hanna Olsson, contacted me recently after reading Stieg's essay on honor crimes to tell me that she would have loved to work with him. Every violent act in *The Millennium Trilogy* was inspired by real murders described in police reports. In Sweden, once sentence is pronounced, the files enter the public domain and may be consulted.

What more beautiful homage could Stieg pay to women than to make them heroines in a feminist crime novel? And to show them as he saw them: brave, free, strong enough to change their world and refuse to be victims. As for the murderers, Stieg's indictment of them in the trilogy is encoded in verses from the Bible.

At the Heart of the Bible

THE REMARKABLE atmosphere Stieg created in *The Millennium Trilogy*, with its characteristic moral rigor and wealth of biblical references, is the one that permeated our early years in Västerbotten County. It's an atmosphere far removed from that of classic crime novels, but one favored by our great writers, such as Per Olov Enquist, the author of *The Royal Physician's Visit*, or Torgny Lindgren, who wrote *The Way of a Serpent*. Both of these men, like Stieg, came from that isolated region in northern Sweden.

Historically speaking, the rest of the country had been under the authority of the Lutheran Church since the sixteenth century, but in the North, dissident and extremely austere Protestant movements sprang up in the nineteenth century, notably the Religious Awakening led by the radical pastor Lars Levi Laestadius. The mission of such movements was to save the populace—mainly workers and peasants—from the ravages of alcoholism. Music and dancing were forbidden, women were not allowed to wear makeup, and so on. These breakaway movements mostly disappeared by the mid-twentieth century, after the advent of the industrial society and massive urbanization.

The world of my childhood was peopled by dissident, conservative country folk who belonged to SEM (the Swedish Evangelical Mission), while Stieg's youth was instead dominated by communist and Social Democratic workers, but all of these people—obstinate, loyal, honest, with a deep sense of morality—were much alike.

Founded in 1856, SEM is a movement dedicated to the renewal of faith within the Lutheran Church. One of its founders, the great lay preacher and author Carl Olof Rosenius, was born in Anäset in Västerbotten County, where my paternal grandmother grew up. One of SEM's articles of faith is that every Christian must live in a direct relationship with God, taking full responsibility for his or her actions—a relationship that begins, of course, in daily life. Since a personal reading of the Bible is one of the essential pillars of religious observance, the movement has always had a strong focus on literacy and education, and one of its major concerns has been the dissemination of religious texts. In 1868, the door-to-door salesmen who handled that task received the authorization to preach, and their influence is still felt today in the region where Stieg and I grew up, which is sometimes called the Bible Belt, like its namesake in the United States. SEM collected money to provide for the work of its preachers and missionaries in Africa and Asia, so even as a child, I was aware of our responsibility toward these continents.

Every village had its small congregation houses where the villagers gathered. Because of the great distances to be traveled, however, people out in the countryside could not attend church regularly, so their pastors and lay preachers, who were sometimes their neighbors, would visit them. And if there was only one book in the house, it was the Bible. I think that even Stieg's communist grandparents had one. The Bible had been a nurturing presence in their childhood, as it was in the lives of every Swedish citizen, because until 1996, everyone was automatically born a Lutheran in Sweden, where church and state were not separated until 2000.

Life was hard in the North, and not just when a family was visited by illness or death; the Bible brought courage and comfort to people who struggled daily to survive in the fields, forests, and the few factories there. For Stieg and me, the Bible was not so much the New Testament, the Jesus who asks us to turn the other cheek, but the formidable Old Testament, blunt and violent, like the age-old way of life up in our territory. Without officials or judges, and with mostly itinerant pastors, society had no fixed hierarchy, so people had to shape rules for themselves in order to survive together. That was the context in which Stieg and I were raised by our grandparents, who lived by the values of older times, and this upbringing gave us a strong moral compass, a faculty doubtless more developed in us than it is in most people of our generation. Some things are done and others are not. Period.

We were not believers, but when we traveled we always visited churches and cemeteries. I loved—and still do—to light candles in memory of the loved ones I have lost.

In our apartment in Stockholm, we each had a Bible that, like the Koran, was always somewhere among our clutter of books. Stieg used his, of course, to help him write about the murders of the young women in the first volume of the trilogy: taking inspiration from real police reports, he then culled from the Bible the verses he could use to create an enigma.

The Duty of Vengeance

STIEG WAS a generous man, loyal, warmhearted, and fundamentally kind. But he could also be completely the opposite. Whenever someone treated him or anyone close to him badly, it was "an eye for an eye, a tooth for a tooth." He never forgave such an affront, and made no bones about it. "To exact revenge for yourself or your friends," he used to say, "is not only a right, it's an absolute duty." Even if he sometimes had to wait for years, Stieg always paid people back.

In the first volume of the trilogy, Henrik Vanger speaks for Stieg when he tells Mikael Blomkvist, "I've had many enemies over the years. If there's one thing I've learned, it's never get in a fight you're sure to lose. On the other hand, never let anyone who has insulted you get away with it. Bide your time and strike back when you're in a position of strength—even if you no longer need to strike back." In the third book, *The Girl Who Kicked the Hornet's Nest*, Mikael explains to Anders Jonasson, the doctor who takes care of Lisbeth Salander, that he must help his young patient even if it's illegal to do so, because he may in good conscience break the law to obey *a higher morality*. For Stieg, Lisbeth was the ideal incarnation of the code of ethics that requires us to act according to our convictions. She is a kind of biblical archangel, the instrument of *The Vengeance of God*, the working title of the fourth volume in *The Millennium Trilogy*.

When he was a boy in Umeå, Stieg got into fights everywhere and often. One day a boy broke one of his front teeth, so Stieg had to have a gold false tooth implanted in his jaw. Long afterward, he lay in wait for his attacker one night and took him by surprise. Stieg never had another problem with him—or anyone else. Yes, revenge is indeed a dish best eaten cold.

This dilemma between morality and action is in fact what drives the plot in *The Millennium Trilogy*. Individuals change the world and their fellow human beings for better or for worse, but each of us acts according to his or her own sense of morality, which is why everything comes down in the end to personal responsibility.

The trilogy allowed Stieg to denounce everyone he loathed for their cowardice, their irresponsibility, and their opportunism: couch-potato activists, sunny-day warriors, fair-weather skippers who pick and choose their causes;

false friends who used him to advance their own careers; unscrupulous company heads and shareholders who wangle themselves huge bonuses. . . . Seen in this light, Stieg couldn't have had any better therapy for what ailed his soul than writing his novels.

Addresses in *The Millennium Trilogy*

IN *THE Girl Who Played with Fire*, Stieg describes what Erika Berger's husband, Lars Beckman, has been doing for the previous six months. An art historian and a successful author, Beckman has been "working on a book about the artistic decoration of buildings and its influences, and why people felt a sense of well-being in some buildings but not in others. The book had begun to develop into an attack on functionalism." With those words Stieg has also summarized the theme of my book on Per Olof Hallman, an architect and urbanist who died in 1941. Stockholm was built on fourteen islands connected by bridges, and Hallman planned residential communities there that accentuated the capital's distinctive greenery, islet rocks, and culturally distinctive houses offering views of the water. Hallman paid particular attention to the *human habitat* through the integration of green spaces, for example, and playgrounds, or even works of art. For Hallman, the goals of architecture and urbanism were to bring people serenity and joie de vivre, for he felt that the environment in which they lived could either strengthen or stress them.

I had begun writing my book in 1997 but was obliged to set it aside when the Swedish government hired me to join a study on the feasibility of constructing affordable quality housing. In 2002, however, I decided to become a part-time consultant so that I could concentrate on my research, which involved spending a great deal of time studying documents in libraries, archives, and stores specializing in old books. Every evening, when Stieg came home and dumped his backpack in the hall, he would always call out, "Hey there! Anybody home?" Then he would head straight for the settee where I sat working and ask his other eternal questions: "What did you find out today? Is there any coffee?" He'd settle in next to me, asking lots of questions and listening closely to my replies.

Since Stieg didn't have time to read each new version of my book, I discussed the text with him regularly. On Saturdays I'd take him on lengthy walks through the "Hallman zones" I was writing about. As a research shortcut for the trilogy (and to give a little nod to my work), he'd asked me if he could use the places I was showing him so that his characters could live in neighborhoods that matched their personalities. That's why Dag Svensson and Mia Bergman—an investigative reporter and a grad student—live in the garden village Enskede, at 8B Björneborgsvägen Street, while Cortez, a reporter for *Millennium*, is on bohemian Alhelgonagatan, in Helgalunden, a neighborhood on Södermalm. And when the trilogy opens, Lisbeth Salander's place is on working-class Lundagatan.

However, Stieg wanted Mikael Blomkvist's apartment to be in the oldest part of Södermalm, not in those Hallman zones. We investigated numerous addresses before finding the right one. Bellmansgatan offered several possibilities, one of which was the Laurinska building, at Nos. 4–6. Since its construction in 1891, many artists had lived in this large red-brick apartment house with its spectacular view over the Riddarfjärden, a bay of Lake Mälaren in central Stockholm, but it was too luxurious for Mikael, who could not have afforded to buy anything there. We next seriously considered what looked to us like the ideal apartment building, with a small view of the bay, but it didn't have enough exits to support the moment in the trilogy when three different groups can all keep Blomkvist under surveillance at the same time. Stieg was disappointed about that, but I told him it wasn't important: "We'll put an imaginary door there"—I pointed to the place—"and give the building a fictitious number. That way, the address will fit the plot."

Stieg's face lit up. "Yes, that's what we'll do!" But somehow that made-up number disappeared in the published version of the surveillance episode, which takes place in the third volume—and Stieg never had time to review any proofs except those for the first book.

At the beginning of *The Girl with the Dragon Tattoo*, Mikael Blomkvist tells how he renovated his apartment himself and hid the worst patches of wall behind two watercolors by Emanuel Bernstone. I've always been very fond of that artist's oeuvre, and at a time when he was completely unknown I bought one of his works, a picture of a red-tailed bird, with my small inheritance from my grandmother. And I was able to buy the second painting, a seagull, with the money left to me by my mother. Both watercolors are strong yet delicate "portraits" of shorebirds, and they have a great serenity. They still hang in the home I shared with Stieg.

For my book on Hallman, I had a lengthy interview with his daughter, who was ninety-six years old at the time. She told me that her father had often gone sailing with Anders Zorn, one of Sweden's foremost painters, and Albert Engström, a prominent Swedish cartoonist and humor writer. The three of them used to drink so much beer that the wharf in front of Hallman's summer home on Skarpö island became littered with empties, and the ferry had trouble unloading its passengers—an anecdote that found its way into the first volume of the trilogy, when Fredrik Vanger and his wife Ulrika go boating with the two artists.

Stieg was so enthusiastic about my Hallman book that he kept telling me confidently, "You'll see, this book is going to change your life." The irony is that it wasn't my book that turned my life upside down, but *The Millennium Trilogy*.

When Lisbeth Salander returns from Grenada at the beginning of the second novel and looks for an apartment, she has plenty of money but still has trouble finding what she wants. Stieg also spent some time looking for that apartment. Actually, I was the one who found it . . . in my research files. At the time I was working at Skanska, the largest construction company in Sweden, so I was naturally interested in everything that concerned the firm. I gathered information about both its construction activities and its chairman of the board, Percy Barnevik, whose enormous pension payouts, accumulated thanks to all of the top executive positions he'd held during his career, had been made public in the media—a revelation I found worrisome both as a citizen and as a salaried employee. When Barnevik sold his apartment on Fiskargatan, I'd filed away a relevant newspaper article that included a floor plan of the place. That's how Lisbeth moved into her lovely apartment on Fiskargatan, near Mosebacke, an area with many cultural venues in the upscale Södermalm district.

Actually, so many of Stieg's characters live and work in Södermalm that this large island, one of the most densely populated districts of the capital, becomes a character in its own right, a part of central Stockholm that is also central to the plot of *The Millennium Trilogy*. Connected on its northern rim to Gamla Stan (the Old Town) by Slussen, a transportation grid with a lock between the Baltic Sea and Lake Mälaren, "Söder" is also linked by bridges to big Kungsholmen to the northwest, little Reimersholme to the west—in fact to a whole ring of islands large and small. In the seventeenth century, rich people began building summer homes in rural, agricultural Södermalm, and working-class housing was built, such as the red cottages still seen today in the northeast of the island. Urbanization proceeded apace in the twentieth century, but as often happens, the by now largely working-class district eventually became home to students, bohemians, and creative souls of all types, and Södermalm currently offers many cultural (and countercultural) amenities. True to form, gentrification brought a new cachet to Söder—and Lisbeth Salander to her apartment at 9 Fiskargatan, thanks to that article in my files.

My documentation also inspired the Skanska stock-options affair at the beginning of *The Girl with the Dragon Tattoo* and the pension scandal at ABB, which Mikael Blomkvist and Robert Lindberg discuss when they meet on the wharf on Arholma, the northernmost island in the Stockholm archipelago. It's after this unfortunate conversation that Blomkvist begins investigating Wennerström and winds up convicted of defamation.

Stieg and I knew all of the cafés that appear in *The Millennium Trilogy*. We used to meet in some of them after work, as we did at the Kafé Anna in Kungsholmen, where Blomkvist hears on the radio that Wennerström has won his libel case. We liked to visit other cafés on the spur of the moment, like the Giffy and the Java on one of Södermalm's main streets, Hornsgatan, perhaps after one of our art gallery expeditions on the Hornsgatan "hill." *Expo*'s informal headquarters were the Kaffebar right downstairs in the same building, where Blomkvist learns—again, on the radio—that the man who tried to murder Lisbeth has himself been murdered. The Kaffebar still serves a marvelous little sandwich made with cheese from Västerbotten County, where Stieg and I grew up. We'd have one of those with our caffe lattes after a visit to our favorite bookstore, a treasure trove of old volumes and books on feminism, politics, and so forth. Kvarnen ("The Mill") is a bustling, noisy restaurant where Lisbeth Salander meets her women friends in the hard rock group Evil Fingers. Kvarnen served delicious meatballs that disappeared at one point from the menu, but the restaurant regulars protested until the owner reinstated these favorites.

Finally, among the many places in the trilogy that belonged to Stieg and me, one I particularly cherish is the little cabin at Sandhamn ("Sand Harbor") where Mikael Blomkvist goes "to read, write, and relax." Every summer we would rent one of these wooden cottages out in the archipelago. Our dream was to build one just for ourselves, and we wanted it to resemble the one described by Lisbeth Salander: about 325 square feet arranged like a boat's cabin, with a large window looking out over the water and a big kitchen table where both of us could write.

The Characters

IN *THE Millennium Trilogy* some real people appear, so to speak, under their own names, because Stieg wanted to honor them in this way. Other people provided real-life details that inspired Stieg when he created his fictional characters out of this and that. And some readers simply think they recognize real people—even themselves—in characters who are wholly imaginary. A plastic surgeon wrote me, for example, that he was convinced he'd been the model for the doctor who enlarges Lisbeth Salander's breasts in *The Girl Who Played with Fire!*

MIKAEL BLOMKVIST is not Stieg Larsson. Like Stieg, he's constantly drinking coffee, smoking, and working like a fiend, but the resemblance basically stops there. On the other hand, though, Blomkvist does clearly embody the figure of the celebrated all-around journalist Stieg would have liked to be, and this character is a spokesperson for many of Stieg's opinions and causes. Blomkvist is also, like his creator, an incorrigible and incorruptible fighter for justice.

◉

IS LISBETH Salander a feminine double for Stieg? The two share the same lousy eating habits, at least, given their addiction to frozen pizzas and fast-food sandwiches. A champion hacker, a prodigy of computer and investigative skills, Lisbeth is blessed with a photographic memory that allows her to memorize complex texts, such as a treatise on spherical astronomy, with dazzling speed. I've already touched on Stieg's incredible memory, his iconoclastic culture, and his inexhaustible hunger for reading about the most varied subjects. Some of the elements in the hacker circles in which Lisbeth moves may come, for example, from *The Hacker Crackdown* by Bruce Sterling, but we also had plenty of *Superman* and *Spider-Man* comics around the house, featuring superheroes with extraordinary powers for whom Lisbeth could serve as a little sister. As for her mania for caution and secrecy, Stieg was the same way—but so was everyone at *Searchlight* and *Expo*, because that wariness came with the territory.

◙

IN *THE Girl Who Played with Fire*, Lisbeth visits her former guardian Holger Palmgren in a rehabilitation home, where they play a rather complicated game of chess, a variant of one of Lasker's most famous games. My brother Björn has a large chess library, including several studies of a few classic games by Emanuel Lasker, the famous German mathematician and chess champion. From the moment they met in the 1970s, Stieg and my brother liked to play chess with each other. Stieg usually lost, but since he wasn't the type to give up, he never refused a rematch. When he left for Africa in 1977, he specified in an unwitnessed will—about which I'll have more to say later—that if he did not return, he wished my brother to inherit all his science fiction books.

Many people think they "recognize" Lisbeth Salander. Some insist she was a journalist who worked at *Expo*. As for Stieg's brother Joakim, he claims she's based on his own daughter, with whom Stieg allegedly communicated by email. Joakim was careful to mention in an interview that these emails just happen to have disappeared somehow in a hard disk crash. . . .

If Lisbeth takes after anyone, it's Pippi Longstocking, our national heroine conjured up by children's book author Astrid Lindgren. This delightful and formidable little girl has been a champion of equality between the sexes: she doesn't depend on anyone, can use a revolver, has sailed the seven seas, and not only can she beat Mighty Adolf, the strongest man in the world . . . she can lift up her pet horse! But the main thing about Pippi is that she has her own ideas about right and wrong—and she lives by them, no matter what the law or adults say. After one of her adventures, she announces, "When I grow up, I'm going to be a pirate." One evening toward the end of the 1990s, Stieg and some journalists at TT had fun imagining what all the favorite storybook idols of Swedish children might really have grown up to be. Pippi Longstocking? Lisbeth Salander, perhaps. And what about Kalle Blomkvist (or Bill Bergson, as he's known in English), the young hero of Astrid Lindgren's trilogy about an ordinary boy who loves to solve mysteries and even real crimes that baffle the police and other adults? Maybe Mikael Blomkvist. The readers of *The Millennium Trilogy* may decide for themselves. Actually, the only *real* Lisbeth Salander in Sweden, who is sixty years old and lives off in a remote village, wrote me to say she was fed up with reporters calling her to ask if she knew Stieg Larsson. She signed off by saying, "If you ever get up this way, come have coffee with me, we'll have a chat and a laugh!"

THE WOMEN in history who interested Stieg were those who defied all stereotypes of "the weaker sex," and he mentions some of them on the first page of *The Girl Who Kicked the Hornet's Nest*: the Amazons, and the women who disguised themselves as soldiers to fight in the American Civil War, and women who led their people to battle like

Boudicca (aka Boadicea), the queen of the Iceni tribe who led a revolt against the Romans in England. On one of the many trips we made to London (especially during the eight years my sister Britt lived there), Stieg took me to Westminster Bridge to show me the statue of Boudicca, one of his favorite heroines.

Erika Berger, the editor in chief of *Millennium*, was entirely made up. That the position is held by a woman is neither an accident nor a literary artifice; in fact I'd have been astonished if Stieg had done otherwise. Erika Berger is competent and assumes full responsibility for both her colleagues and the finances of the magazine. Her private life is rather unconventional, in that she has a husband and a lover, and she acts on her desires, which does cause her some problems.

For some aspects of Anita Vanger, Stieg drew on my sister Britt. While he was writing the first book, he asked her if, "as" Anita, she would like to live in Guildford, southwest of London, where she lived after she first moved to England from Sweden, but Britt preferred to go north instead, to "a terrace house in the attractive suburb of St. Albans." Throughout her London years, Britt always lived in apartments heated by gas radiators set into fireplaces, an arrangement Stieg and I knew well. Whenever we arrived at my sister's place, we'd rush to turn on the heat, relieved to see the temperature rise beyond the 60 degrees Fahrenheit Britt had finally gotten used to!

Sometimes, like Martina Karlgren or Franck Ellis in *The Girl Who Kicked the Hornet's Nest*, a character in the trilogy mentions scientific or professional journals such as *Nature* or *The New England Journal of Medicine*, which Britt read in conjunction with her work in medical research. She often told us about articles she'd found particularly interesting, so Stieg was quite familiar with such publications.

Giving some of his characters real people's names, and even their professions or personalities, was for Stieg a mark of affection and admiration. We didn't know the boxer Paolo Roberto personally, but in Sweden he's a celebrity. Although he was a young delinquent in the 1980s, he then became a professional boxer and in 1987 played the lead in a film loosely dramatizing his early life: Staffan Hildebrand's *Stockholmsnatt* (*Stockholm Night* or *The King of Kungsan*), an important cult film in Sweden. Today Paolo Roberto has a cooking show on television—and his Italian aunts don't hesitate to grab a spoon out of his hands when he isn't stirring tomato sauce the right way! Stieg was especially impressed by Roberto's frankness, and his unpredictability. He can be totally macho one minute and then suddenly begin championing equality between the sexes. During the 2002 elections, he almost got into Parliament, but came in second. On the other hand, he did make it into *The Millennium Trilogy*.

▣

THE PSYCHIATRIST Svante Branden, who helps Lisbeth Salander defend herself against Dr. Peter Teleborian in the third volume, is one of our old friends. I've already mentioned that I sublet his student room when I arrived in Stockholm in

1977, before Stieg had found his job with the postal service and come to join me. Like us, Svante Branden has always been against all forms of discrimination and abuse. As a psychiatrist, he's particularly skilled at perceiving people's real motives behind whatever smoke screen of excuses they may make. Stieg wanted to pay homage to him by casting him as an "ordinary hero" in daily life. After Stieg's death, however, and the behavior of his father and brother regarding the moral, intellectual, and material legacy of my partner (about which I'll have more to say later), Svante no longer felt honored to be in the trilogy. And he wrote to the Larssons to tell them why.

As a specialist in legal psychiatry, I firmly wish my name to be associated with justice and morality. That Stieg should want to borrow my name for his book was an honor for me. But after his death, you, Joakim, are profiting from Stieg's work and you are using my name without my authorization. Although your strange—to say the least—statements to the press about Stieg and Eva are no doubt protected by law, they smack of a morality fit for a profiteer and a corrupt accountant. For this reason I require that you remove my name from Stieg's book immediately and that you pay me damages for having profited from my name and professional standing.

Given that Stieg wished to see my name in his book, my demands are modest: a lump sum of 32 kronor. In addition, I will ask for 1 krona* per year until you come to some agreement with Eva. As of today, the sum owed comes to 36 kronor. You may transfer the money to my account at Handelsbanken.

---

*15 cents

The Larssons sent their answer directly to the editors of *Uppdrag Granskning* (*Mission: Investigation*), a serious television program on investigative journalism, who published it on their website. Svante then allowed the editors to publish his own letter on the website of Swedish National Television. In the Larssons' letter, Stieg's brother proposed sarcastically that Svante might be of some psychiatric help to me—and offered to donate all damages asked to charity. . . .

◻

IN STIEG'S manuscript, Anders Jakobsson is the doctor who admits Lisbeth Salander to the emergency room of Sahlgrenska University Hospital in Gothenburg at the beginning of *The Girl Who Kicked the Hornet's Nest*. He operates, removes the bullet lodged in her brain, and saves her life. All through her hospitalization, which lasts for dozens and dozens of pages, he helps her. He talks to her, listens to her, sneaks her Palm Tungsten T3 personal digital assistant to her, and so forth. Anders had been a friend to Stieg and me ever since the Umeå years of the 1970s. In 2006, at Eastertime—after Stieg had died and his father and brother had begun to stop considering me Stieg's legitimate widow—Anders ran into Erland in a small supermarket in Umeå and did not conceal his opinion about the matter. After that incident, the Larssons had Norstedts Förlag, the publishers of the trilogy, change "Anders Jakobsson" to "Anders Jonasson" in the third book of the trilogy! This

The wooden house of Stieg Larsson's maternal grandparents in Västerbotten County, northern Sweden.

NORSJÖ KOMMUN

BETYGSBOK

för

Stig Larsson
Pjäsön

NORSJÖ KOMMUN   Års-nr 46/54
Betygsbok
(terminsintyg och terminsbetyg)
för
Karl Stig Erland Larsson
Född den *15 aug.* 19 *54*
i *Skellefteå stad, Västerbottens län*
          stad eller församling och län
Målsman: *Severin Boström*

Målsmans bostad: *Pjäsön*
Eleven inskriven i *Pjäsöns* ~~försöksskola~~ folkskola
av *Norsjö* kommun

Stieg Larsson's grandparents "in disguise," sitting in front of their house with his grandmother's sister in 1958.

Left: The interior of the little wooden house.

Right: One of Stieg Larsson's report cards, on which his grandfather, Severin Boström, is designated as the boy's guardian.

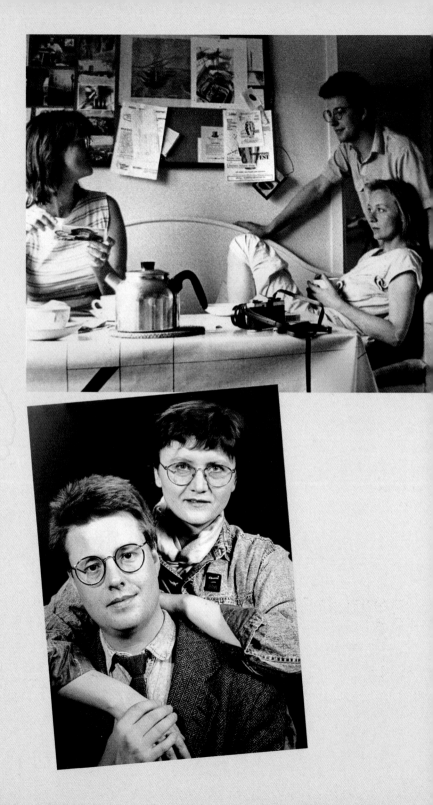

Top left: Eva Gabrielsson and Stieg Larsson with Eva's sister, Britt, in their apartment in Rinkeby in 1985.

Above: The inaugural issue of the magazine *Expo*, 1995. In this issue:
    The Swedish Far-Right: Seven Deaths Already This Year
    The Nazi Intelligence Network in Sweden
    Anti-Semitism: Who is Desecrating Jewish Graves?
    Is White Power Music Financing Neo-Nazism?
    Death in Oklahoma
    Michael Schmidt: Do We Really Need Expo?
    Schools as Recruitment Centers

Bottom left: Portrait of Eva Gabrielsson and Stieg Larsson in the mid-1990s.

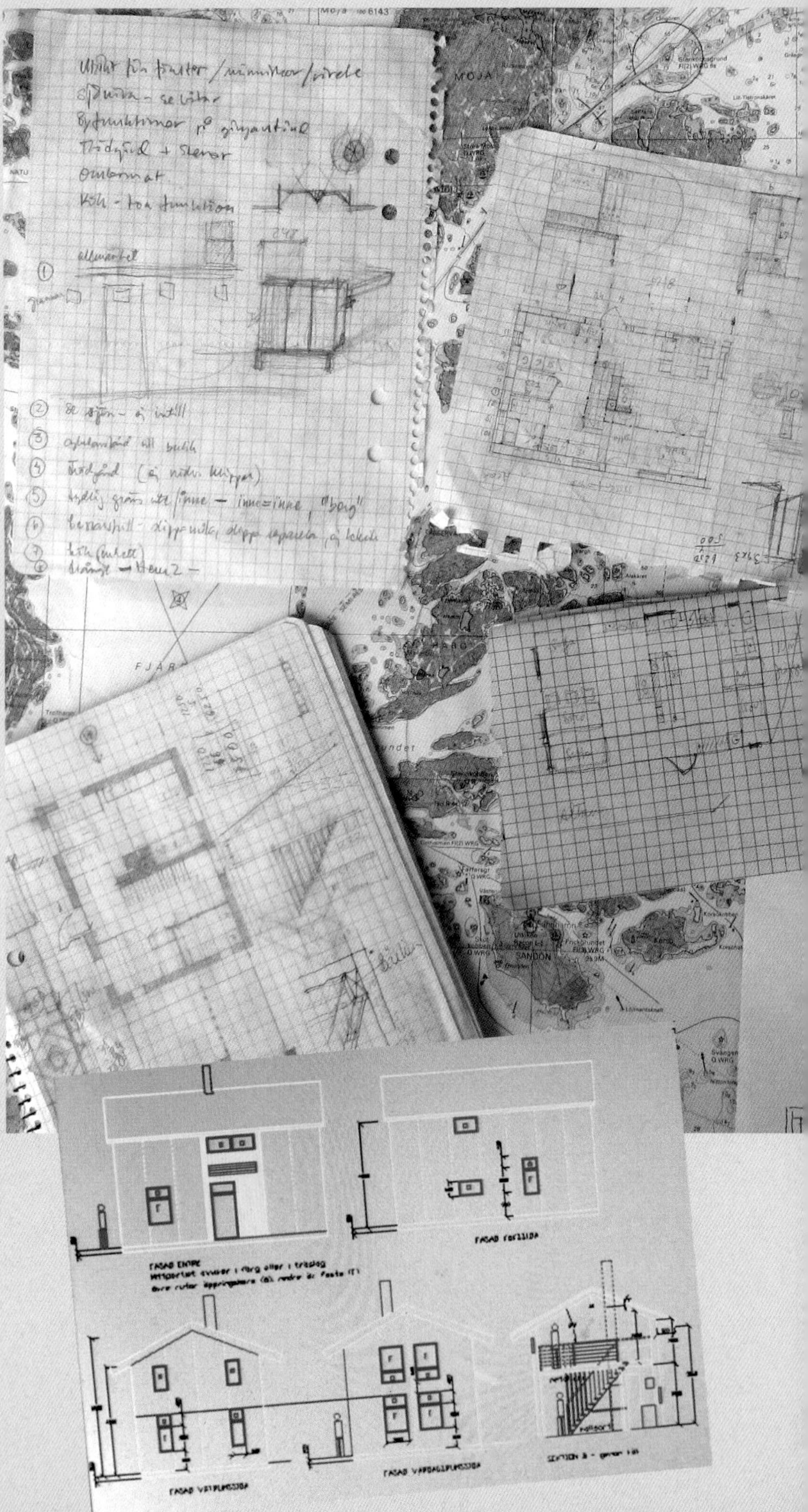
MÖJA
SANDÖN

Top right: Map of the Stockholm archipelago, the favorite sailing grounds of Stieg Larsson and Eva Gabrielsson.

Left: Sketches for the "writing cottage" of Stieg Larsson and Eva Gabrielsson.

Above: Photo of Stieg Larsson taken by Eva Gabrielsson in the Stockholm archipelago, 1990.

Eva Gabrielsson and Stieg Larsson in 1980.

December 10, 2004: Eva Gabrielsson at the commemoration for Stieg Larsson.

story was confirmed by Norstedts and the Larssons on camera in an interview for "The Millennium Millions," a program broadcast on *Uppdrag Granskning* in the spring of 2008. Anders Jakobsson then sent a letter to one of the journalists, which is posted on the Swedish National Television website.

Dear Fredrik Quistbergh,

Norstedts has now confirmed that Stieg Larsson's manuscript was altered before publication.

To mix real people in with fictitious characters was an important literary concept in Stieg Larsson's novels. With the help of Norstedts, Erland and Joakim Larsson have interfered with Stieg Larsson's original manuscript by changing the names of certain people in the third book.

This is a serious violation of Stieg Larsson's work and his intentions. The motive for this intervention can be clearly seen in the interview Erland Larsson gave to Uppdrag Granskning: *"Petty or vindictive, call it what you like, but that's what we decided."*

For more than thirty years, Stieg Larsson lived with his companion Eva Gabrielsson in a relationship that was in all ways like marriage. Erland and Joakim Larsson have now seized permanent control of Stieg Larsson's estate as well as the intellectual and moral rights to his work. The law is serving a deeply immoral cause. It is flagrantly obvious to all of the friends of Stieg Larsson that such behavior is immoral. Erland Larsson's indignation at my remarks on this point clearly show that this is a touchy subject for him—which is without doubt proof that Erland Larsson is perfectly aware that it is morally deplorable to deprive Eva Gabrielsson of

the estate of her companion, Stieg. I met Stieg when we were in
high school back in Umeå. We were very close for more than thirty
years. So I can affirm that Stieg would never have allowed any-
one to distort his books or deprive his companion Eva of her in-
heritance. In fact, if he were alive, Stieg would have done all he
could to stop this. And he would have stopped at nothing.

Sincerely yours,
Anders Jakobsson

Another everyday heroine in our personal pantheon who
shows up in *The Millennium Trilogy* is the woman who saved
a man named Joy Rahman. In *The Girl Who Played with Fire*,
when Mikael and police inspector Jan Bublanski argue
about whether Lisbeth is really implicated in the murders
of Dag Svensson and Mia Bergman, Blomkvist brings up
a miscarriage of justice that is quite well-known in Sweden,
the case of Joy Rahman. This man was condemned and imprisoned for the murder of an elderly lady and would still
be behind bars if a teacher at his children's school had not
devoted several years to an assiduous investigation of his
case. Stieg and I knew this teacher and understood her
anger, and as we followed her struggle, we were appalled
by the flaws she uncovered in the Swedish justice system.
Our admiration grew for this stubborn woman who simply
would not give up: she managed to have new forensic tests
conducted, and with the help of a good lawyer, a psychiatrist, the prison chaplain, and a journalist, she gathered
enough proof to obtain a new trial for Rahman, who was

found innocent and set free after eight years in prison. In 2003, she and the journalist were awarded the Democracy Prize by Örebro University in Sweden. This schoolteacher well deserves her place in *The Millennium Trilogy*.

Grenada

THE FIRST hundred pages of *The Girl Who Played with Fire* take place on the island of Grenada, where Lisbeth has decided to spend some time. Why Grenada? Because it was our island. And that's a long story.

Early in the 1980s, Stieg and I happened to read some articles by African American journalists about the Grenadian people in the English-language magazine of the Fourth International, in which there was an entertaining account of the popular uprising that toppled the dictator Eric Gairy, who had often deeply embarrassed his country before the entire world . . . *in speeches full of references to UFOs*, in which he adamantly believes.

This spot far across the ocean intrigued us. With its crazy

mix of social democracy and Trotskyism, it seemed to enjoy a humanist attitude graced with something of a sense of humor. Stieg and I spent the summer of 1981 on this island dominated by its slumbering volcano, with its roads flanked by dense jungle. Flying out of Luxemburg, we first touched down, like Lisbeth, in Barbados, where we changed planes to a puddle jumper. The pilot, a charming Rasta with long dreadlocks, landed on a tiny runway threading between beach and mountainside. We stayed at a place called Seascape, uphill from the wharf where ships docked, and we liked to stroll along the beach at Grand Anse, where the sand was as fine as powder and we could dive through shoals of colorful fish. But we were not on vacation, oh no. We were eager to write about what was happening there, so we lost no time in making appointments with political figures. At the Ministry of Tourism, we learned that an ecotourism project was under consideration, involving small hotels integrated into the landscape and the local habitat, and meals based on local products. I remember in particular a conversation about shopkeepers who wanted to raise their prices outrageously. We were on their side and found that normal, since Grenada, like the rest of the Caribbean, must import almost everything, from auto parts to toilet paper. Stieg and I came up with a sensible solution: the implementation of two price systems, one more expensive than the other. It would be up to tourists and the more well-off islanders to choose a system in accordance with their means and their desire to help the population. Not a very practical concept, but it was certainly interesting to think about!

We would have liked to live there for years, but when that summer was over, we had to leave. As soon as we got home we contacted the Grenada Support Committee, and the Grenadian consul in Sweden, Eleanor Raiper, became a dear friend. We had wonderful times together, because Grenadians are jolly, fun-loving people who don't get all bogged down in grandiose theories the way some of our friends do. We started a magazine, and to raise funds for the island cooperatives, we didn't go door-to-door the way we used to, but instead organized "dinner-dances" where Caribbean food was served. A delightful way to practice politics!

In the fall of 1983, the United States invaded Grenada. Since I was working with Stieg at TT at the time to earn a little money, we heard the news as soon as it came over the wire. Then I remembered that when the Soviets invaded Czechoslovakia in 1968, my father, who was a journalist, had had the bright idea of calling the hotels there. That's how he quickly obtained eyewitness information, making his local paper the only one in the country to publish such scoops. Thanks to Eleanor, who had a Grenadian phone book, Stieg and I were able to pull off the same coup: TT was the only media outlet to provide interviews right away. When we learned that over 10,000 American soldiers had landed on our island, I burst into tears. Sweden hadn't had a war in over two hundred years, and I somehow imagined that all 110,000 Grenadians were going to be massacred.

The description in *The Millennium Trilogy* of the rise and fall of the government of Maurice Bishop, the charismatic leader of the New Jewel movement, is of course the result of everything we saw on the island and learned later on. Writing about Grenada was a way of paying tribute to people who had given us much, and with whom we had been happy.

Sailing

IN *THE Millennium Trilogy*, it's no accident that for Mikael Blomkvist, everything begins on a boat. Water and the sea are inescapable when you live in a country with almost 13,000 miles of coastline and thousands of small islands.

The Stockholm archipelago is the largest one we have in Sweden, and every year Stieg and I would set off to explore one of its 24,000 islands. In the North, where we were born, we rowed our boats, since sailing was considered a sport for snobs. So before tackling a trip during which we might sink, drown, or be knocked cold by a swinging boom, I'd managed to get Stieg to join me in a crash course in sailing. He adored studying charts, having learned map reading during his military service. Me, I preferred to be at the helm. We'd take turns there, but if the weather worsened, I'd take over the wheel. We started out by buying *Josephine*, and we kept that name because a change would have brought bad luck. She was a secondhand motorboat, mahogany, twenty-eight feet, built in 1954, the year Stieg was born. When we began sailing, however, we always rented our boats. As a pair we functioned perfectly well, almost via osmosis. Once, whipped by a ferocious wind, the boom broke loose, and as our friend Eleanor watched in amazement, Stieg and I immediately cobbled together an emergency tie-up with some military webbing belts—without needing to exchange a single word.

Josephine's home port was Årsta, where Mikael goes to exchange Christmas presents with his ex-wife and daughter Pernilla in *The Girl with the Dragon Tattoo*. Thanks to all our trips back and forth, Stieg and I knew the area well.

When Lisbeth decides to strong-arm her way into the apartment of Per-Åke Sandström, the pimp "journalist" who is Dag Svensson's informant, she equips herself at Watski, a hardware store on Erstagatan in Stockholm. That was where Stieg and I bought everything we needed for boating. I particularly remember an anchor and chain that must have weighed more than sixty-five pounds, and which I lugged through the Årsta forest all the way to *Josephine*.

To tie up Sandström, Lisbeth uses a clove hitch, a knot Stieg and I tied and retied for whole evenings to get right. As for her little Minolta 8x binoculars, they're the ones we always had in our pockets when we were sailing, to help us spot seamarks and stay on course.

We knocked around quite a lot at the top of the archipelago, too, up by Arholma, the most northerly island, where Blomkvist meets the old school chum who gives him the idea to write about Wennerström. The guest marina there is as busy as Stieg says, and boats really have to crowd together to leave a few spaces for latecomers. I've never understood the strange popularity of the place, because it's the favorite summer resort of enormous mosquitoes, twice as big as normal, which feast on visitors all night long.

After Holger Palmgren retired, the lawyer Nils Erik Bjurman became Lisbeth's legal guardian, and this vile character owns a second home in Stallarholmen. Stieg and I often put in there with *Josephine* whenever we were touring Lake Mälaren during the summer.

Bjurman's friend Gunnar Björck, the assistant chief of the immigration division within Säpo and a member of the Section, tries to hide at the end of the trilogy by going way out to Landsort, a village on the island of Öja, where he rents a guest room in an old lighthouse. For several autumns in a row, Stieg and I sailed south along the archipelago, heading for Landsort, and each time we had to cut our trip short because of bad weather. After hours of fighting gray seas and contrary winds, we'd turn back, discouraged by how little headway we'd made. One summer, frustrated by those setbacks, we took a room in the lighthouse and spent several days there, just so we could finally see the island at least one time!

In the last part of *The Girl Who Kicked the Hornet's Nest*, Mikael has an affair with the stunning Inspector Monica

Figuerola, the Säpo policewoman assigned to Lisbeth Salander's case. While he's staying in the little wooden cabin out at Sandhamn, he goes to get her at the ferry dock, and that same night they have dinner together outside on the veranda. Figuerola questions Blomkvist about his real relationship with Lisbeth, and at one point she watches an Amigo 23 chugging past, heading for the marina with its navigation lights glowing.

One autumn, when rental prices had dropped a bit but the weather had been less cooperative, Stieg and I rented one of these pretty little sailboats with the simply sublime interior finished with precious hardwoods. She was very stable but rather sluggish, especially with the wind astern, which was what we had to deal with for several days. I was grumbling at the helm; *why* had we rented this bathtub that seemed to be dragging an anchor behind her! Then came the day when we suddenly faced a headwind, and to our amazement, the Amigo 23 underwent a sea change: she awakened, sat up, took a deep breath, and began bravely to cleave the waves. She'd become so agile that—remarkably—not one drop of spray touched us! Sheer happiness. I couldn't stop stroking her flanks to thank and encourage her, but she was in her element and no longer needed us at all. Dazzled and dry, we streaked in no time to the far end of the island, absolutely charmed by this Amigo 23 that thoroughly deserved her name.

And that's why Stieg saluted this little boat that gave us such a surprising and fantastic experience.

Schemes and Scams

IN THE 1990s, the banking and real estate debacle described by Mikael Blomkvist and Robert Lindberg at the beginning of *The Girl with the Dragon Tattoo* was a reality with which Stieg and I, unfortunately, were only too familiar.

The financial crisis that affected every industrialized nation hit Sweden particularly hard. To parry a speculative attack on the krona, the Bank of Sweden was forced into a devaluation, which did not help the debt burden of banks that were already in serious trouble.

New taxes, a staggering rise in interest rates, a drop in construction subsidies. . . . The real estate sector took a huge hit, with many firms closing or resorting to massive layoffs. When I lost my job as an architect, Stieg and I entered a period of very tough times.

In the autumn of 1992, Blomkvist says, "I had a variable-rate mortgage on my apartment when the interest rate shot up five hundred percent in October. I was stuck with nineteen percent interest for a year." That is exactly what happened to Sweden, and to us personally. Fortunately, my severance pay helped supply part of the 100,000 extra kronor—almost $15,000—we had to hand over that dreadful year, and if we hadn't paid, we would have lost our home, a 600-square-foot apartment on the top floor of a walk-up. Bought two years earlier in a former working-class neighborhood of Stockholm, it was the first apartment we ever owned. And it is still my home.

◨

IT WASN'T until 1996 that the Swedish government began to worry about a very serious situation: aside from a few superexpensive co-op apartments, housing construction had been more or less at a standstill since 1992. Parliament then launched a vast study of plans for both low-cost housing and research into broad solutions to make the construction sector as a whole more productive and less expensive. I applied for a position in the Construction Cost Delegation, and I was hired. Between 1997 and 2000, I labored day and night over questions that have long interested me and which I had already studied extensively on my own. And now—I was being paid to do that! It was heaven. The project generated over 2,400 pages, and allusions to its contents crop up all through the last volume of *The Millennium Trilogy*. Because Stieg didn't have time to read the whole report, every day for three years I told him highlights of what was in it. Certain details were eye-opening, and even amusing.

For example: "You want to run a story on toilets? In *Millennium*?" exclaims Malin Eriksson, the acting editor in chief of the magazine, in *The Girl Who Kicked the Hornet's Nest*. She can't believe that Henry Cortez, their investigative whiz, wants to write about such a frivolous subject in their distinguished magazine. But wait! The real story is that Swedish construction cartels shamelessly and grossly inflate the prices for cheaply manufactured toilets they buy from Asian countries such as Thailand. The mocking description Stieg concocts about how taxpayers are shafted by such price-fixing really tickled my colleagues at the Construction Cost Delegation, who got the point immediately and recognized data from our study.

◧

IN 2000, Stieg and I were disgusted to learn that leading asphalt paving contractors had formed an "asphalt cartel" that for years had been raking in exorbitant sums for routine road maintenance throughout Sweden. Even worse, the Swedish Road Administration was implicated in the affair, which led the minister of industry at the time to admit that the situation was "embarrassing"! That prompted us to write an article together that only Stieg signed, because of our wish never to have our names linked together. The piece, entitled "Embarrassing? Criminal!," appeared in the national evening paper *Aftonbladet*. And it had repercussions: one municipality sued the contractors for reimbursement of all taxpayers' monies spent, and prices in that sector of construction fell by more than 25 percent.

A result that convinced Stieg and me that we should definitely plan to work together again on issues like these.

Heading for Publication

ON THAT autumn day in 2003, when I walked into our apartment, I remember yelling, "It's just not possible!"

I was returning from the post office, where I'd retrieved the brown-paper-wrapped package containing the manuscript of the first volume of *The Millennium Trilogy*, which Stieg had sent off during the summer to Piratförlaget, Sweden's third-largest publishing house. "They didn't even go pick it up!" I added.

Stieg was bewildered. "But when I called them that day, *they* were the ones who asked me to send it. . . ."

"We're not giving up! Call them back and tell them I'll deliver it to them myself."

A few days later I set out in the rain for Gamla Stan, the

old quarter of Stockholm, with the manuscript wrapped in the same brown paper. A big chunk of book. And I know what I'm talking about: some nights when I used to lie on my bed exhausted after a busy day, pen in hand, with the latest version of the text propped up on my chest, I would doze off . . . and the whole thing would smack mc right in the face!

I delivered the package to a pleasant blonde and was able to assure Stieg that it was now on someone's desk.

But there was no further news. Several weeks went by before Stieg decided to call, only to learn that Piratförlaget wasn't interested.

"Too bad," I announced. "Your book is great, it'll be published someday, and since those people don't seem to know where the post office is, I'm going to go get the book back right now!"

AFTER STIEG'S ritual "Anybody home?" later that same evening, we took a look at the manuscript at around midnight. It was in pristine condition. *Too* pristine. Not one crease, or dog-ear, or even the slightest smudge. . . . It was obvious that no one had opened it.

"I don't get it," Stieg sighed. "Well, what do we care. Never mind. . . . Want any coffee?"

"There's some ready!"

AFTER STIEG'S death and the book's success, a woman called me from Piratförlaget in some despair. She was the one who had received the manuscript and she told me that because of a lack of personnel, a great number of manuscripts had been systematically rejected without being read.

So the first volume of *The Millennium Trilogy* sat out in our hallway for a while, and it was Robert Aschberg, the publisher of *Expo*, who later delivered another copy of the manuscript to Norstedts, Sweden's oldest publishing house, founded in 1823. At the time, Stieg was completely immersed in his work with Cecilia Englund on their anthology about honor killings, and he had other things on his mind. Good news was on the way, however. Not long ago, I came across a letter to Stieg dated March 2004 from the publishing house of Hjalmarsson & Höglund, which would publish the first volume of the trilogy, they said, but only after extensive rewriting. Stieg did not reply. Especially since shortly afterward, in the spring of 2004, Norstedts agreed to publish *The Millennium Trilogy* as is! I remember emailing one of our acquaintances with the news: "Call Stieg to congratulate him—with this success, he's walking on air, and he deserves it so much!"

That April, I began a new job in Falun, the capital of Dalarna County in central Sweden, 150 miles northwest from Stockholm. After many years of working on ways to introduce more efficient and sustainable practices into the construction sector, I now had the chance to try putting such practices into action. Since I was working directly with local construction companies, I was spending four days a week in Falun. One weekend, Stieg told me he'd signed a contract for those first three volumes with an advance of 591,000 kronor (about $86,500). In the letter of confirmation, Norstedts explained to Stieg that like many authors, he could establish a company to which the advance would be paid, and if he wished, an administrator at Norstedts would discuss with him the advantages and disadvantages of various kinds of companies. Enthusiastic about this idea, Stieg told me that Norstedts could help set up some kind of partnership in which I would be a cofounder. I suppose that is why the 591,000 kronor were not paid to Stieg at that time, which would have been the normal thing to do. As for me, knowing how clueless Stieg could be about such things, I figured it made sense that this publishing house would offer to help authors who must all have been as innocent as Stieg in such matters. Did Stieg misunderstand what Norstedts told him? Was it an offer simply to advise him, but not to help him set up the company? In any case, as far as we two were concerned, it was agreed that from then on, everything we earned beyond our salaries—from articles, reports, the royalties from my Hallman book, etc.—would be paid directly to this company. So there was no need, Stieg explained to me, to start dealing with a mass of paperwork like wills, for example, because we would be equal co-owners of everything and the company statutes would stipulate that if one of us died, the other would get everything.

I later checked our inheritance laws and verified this information, and since Stieg himself knew nothing about such things, a lawyer must indeed have spoken to him about them.

Every now and then, I asked him how the setting up of the company was going, and he would tell me that it was being taken care of, that there was no rush. . . .

▣

ONCE STIEG knew his novels would be published, a wonderful period began for us, one of the most beautiful memories of my life.

When I'd get home to Stockholm every Thursday night, Stieg would be waiting in the apartment and dinner would be ready: a simple meal, but home-cooked, like cutlets and green beans. This detail might seem unimportant, but it isn't. Stieg was finally putting our life first. And he was changing the way he ate. The sandwiches, pizzas, junk food—gone. For the first time since I'd known him, he was starting to look after himself. He even bought some omega-3 fish oil supplements! I was beginning to recognize the man I'd met when he was eighteen years old. After all those years of stress, what with his job ending at the news agency TT, and the creation and difficult management of *Expo*, so chronically short of funding, Stieg was at last serene. His novels were going to be published and he was recognized for his true worth. He could breathe easy.

Aside from those few months Stieg spent in Africa, we'd never really been separated during the thirty-two years we'd spent together. So it was a real pleasure to be a couple again after each week spent apart. Stieg had put the word out to his "entourage": "Now I want to spend my weekends with Eva." Putting me first, even before *Expo*, that was an absolute revolution.

We'd always had what was basically a good life together, even during the worst years, but during this period Stieg was full of zest and deeply happy.

We made all sorts of plans.

He was determined to leave his position as editor in chief of *Expo* and to work there only half-time. Once my contract in Falun was over, my intentions were to find a part-time job that would allow us to work together, to add my knowledge to his talent as a writer so we could publish other books. We were especially eager to tackle a subject as yet unexplored: the construction industry. And there'd be more to say there than would fit in an article on crooked asphalt contractors.

We thought *The Millennium Trilogy* would be a hit in the Scandinavian countries and perhaps Germany as well. As we saw it, this popularity would in itself be a kind of protection for Stieg. And we'd be able to appear in public together! What's more, some of the money earned would pay for more sophisticated security when and where we might need it.

So: Stieg had decided that what now came first was us, as a couple. That's why he planned to have the money from the first three novels go toward improving our living situation, the first step of which was to pay off the 440,000 kronor ($64,500) debt remaining on our mortgage. Then we'd agreed to donate the proceeds from the fourth novel to *Expo*, to put the magazine on a solid financial footing and assure its continued publication. The income from the fifth book would be invested in the establishment of safe houses for women victims of violence. As for the other books, there was plenty of time to think about that.

Our absolute dream, as I've already said, was to have—at long last—our own cabin on an island. This would be "our little writing cottage," as we called it, where we'd go regularly to work. And thanks to the publication of the trilogy, this dream was going to come true. To us, this cottage was more than a hideaway; most of all, it was the symbol of a new life. Our chief requirements were modest. Stieg wanted it to be near a café and a place that sold newspapers. I wanted a cabin that was soundly built and easy to maintain. The single thing we both wanted was two wooden settees. Why? At home, the battle for the single one in the living room was escalating into silliness. We could both stretch out on it by facing each other at opposite ends, but as soon as one of us got up, the other would spread out or, even worse, snag the coveted spot over by the corner of the wall. Aside from this most vital detail, we wanted our cabin to be gray, not red in the Swedish style, and the slanting roof was to be covered in sedum, a plant of the Crassulaceae family. Sometimes called stonecrops, these flowering succulents are known especially for their fat, stubby leaves, which provide protection from both heat and cold. I also wanted to use new construction techniques, such as a compact, insulated rubber floor for the bathroom.

We daydreamed for weeks about our paradise, drawing pictures of it while we were apart and then comparing our sketches on weekends.

At the same time, we were also looking for the right piece of property. And later, in the autumn, I would prepare a computer rendition of the final sketch and floor plan for our cabin. (By that time, I'd managed to fit in our two famous settees and even a little corner for overnight guests, so in October I sent the computer proposal to a factory specializing in the construction of "green" houses with a request for a cost estimate.)

The last summer with Stieg was completely different from all the others. Of course, Stieg was very tired, and no wonder: in addition to readying the first volume of the trilogy for publication with Norstedts, he'd been continuing his work at *Expo* and still giving lectures. In June, for example, he'd gone to Paris with a Swedish delegation sent by the Ministry of Justice to a conference on hate crimes and the Internet, organized by the OSCE (Organization for Security and Co-operation in Europe). But now that we had some time to spare, it seemed important to "make the rounds" of our friends. (And after Stieg's death, how thankful we were, our friends and I, that we hadn't postponed our tour until the following year.)

Transformed into a walking travel agency, I busied myself with the itinerary and with organizing our transportation and lodgings. My sister Britt accompanied us to Scania, the province on the southern tip of the

Scandinavian Peninsula, as well as to Gothenburg and the scenic Koster Islands off the west coast of Sweden. It was on this trip that I realized how tired Stieg actually was. When Britt and I would go off for a walk, for example, instead of going with us as usual he would remain at the hotel, reading the papers. I wasn't particularly alarmed, though. For his fiftieth birthday, which we'd recently celebrated in mid-August, my sister had wanted to give him a complete checkup as a present, but since we weren't the kind of people who consult a doctor when they aren't ill, my sister, brother, and I opted in the end for a DVD player. Two months later, we would bitterly regret this.

That summer, Stieg and I wound up our long tour as we always did, in a small rented cottage on the Stockholm archipelago.

One evening, home again at the end of August, when we were sitting close together on our settee, he asked me timidly, "Why don't we get married now?" He'd spoken as if fearing a refusal, but I made a show of my delight, and was also a touch embarrassed, from surprise. We decided that in the autumn we'd give ourselves a huge party for our fiftieth birthdays and then reveal to our friends that it was really our wedding celebration. Ever since a trip to Lisbon in 2001, we'd been saving a bottle of Quinta do Noval Porto 1976 for our fiftieths. But we never had time for either the marriage or the party. That bottle of port turns up in Lisbeth Salander's new apartment in the second book of *The Millennium Trilogy*. Now it's in my kitchen. I will never open it.

During that last summer, the sea was with us everywhere. Those constantly renewed horizons seemed to us the symbol of all the changes ushering in our new life. Well, my life did change. Unfortunately.

November 2004

Monday, November 8

THAT DAY, as always, Stieg was running late. Toward the
end of the morning, he'd gone out to have breakfast in a
café, also as usual, before heading on to *Expo*. I kissed him
goodbye. He was in good spirits. At around a quarter to
eight that evening, I phoned him from the station just to
say hi before my train left Stockholm. He was fine. Three
hours later, I arrived in Falun. It was winter, a dark night,
and I had to make my way through poorly lighted narrow
streets. (I always carried a can of mace.) As soon as I arrived, I called Stieg to tell him all was well; it was one of
our rituals, it reassured him. There was no real news to re-
late. "Lots of love, good night."

◫

Tuesday, November 9

AFTER BREAKFAST, I got a call from Mikael Ekman, a journalist at *Expo*, who told me that Stieg had had some kind of collapse. He advised me to contact Richard, the editorial secretary, at the office. Then Richard explained that Stieg had been taken away in an ambulance, accompanied by Per, a friend of ours whom we've known for thirty years. I called Per, only to learn that the situation was quite serious. When I asked him what I should do, he said: "Get here right away."

I left work immediately, dashed to the station, and took the next train. Since it wasn't an express train, I called Per again when it stopped at Gävle, about a hundred miles north of Stockholm. His voice sounded strange.

"Eva, you have to hurry."

Then I phoned Erland, Stieg's father, in Umeå. His companion, Gun, explained to me that he was at the library doing some genealogical research. I told her that Stieg was in the hospital, I didn't know why, but that it sounded serious and I thought Erland ought to go to Stockholm.

When I arrived at around seven that evening, Per was waiting for me at the entrance to St. Göran's Hospital. Five or six people were with him, including Svante, our psychiatrist friend. They all looked at me in silence. A nurse brought me some coffee, and I went to see a doctor who wanted to speak to me. And then I heard, "I am sorry to have to tell you that your husband has passed away." He told me that Stieg had arrived in serious condition and been immediately taken to radiology, but that since the chest X-rays had been inconclusive, the cardiologist had sent Stieg to an operating room for an interventional procedure. Stieg had then lost consciousness; a few moments later, his heart had stopped beating. For more than forty minutes, the medical team had tried to revive him. In vain.

At 4:22 that afternoon, he was declared dead.

In fact, he was already gone when I'd gotten on the train. When I returned to the waiting room, no one made a sound. I looked at them all. "You knew he was dead the last time I called here?" They nodded. The doctor had advised them not to tell me anything.

I was asked whether I wanted to see Stieg. I was so lost that I even wondered, confusedly, "Should I do that?" And then I thought, yes, because otherwise I would never manage to believe it. I wanted Erland, his father, to be there with me. I called Gun again. "So," she asked cheerfully, "how's Stieg?"

"He's dead," I replied dully. Gun told me Erland had taken a plane to Stockholm. I went to the main hospital entrance to wait for him. Back and forth I went, between the lobby and the sidewalk outside, smoking almost a whole pack of cigarettes. More and more people from *Expo* joined us; some seemed to drift in from the darkness but they stayed outside, completely disoriented and in tears, while others literally burst out of the taxis that brought them. Everyone was hugging, embracing, weeping . . . except for me; I still felt turned to stone. People were in a state of collapse, dazed, at a loss, while I was simply there: I was smoking, and I didn't understand anything. When I looked at that crowd of people in despair, though, I did tell myself that Stieg had had some good and wonderful friends at *Expo*.

That's when I thought to call my sister, my brother, and our great friend Eleanor.

When Erland arrived, I went to meet him and took his arm. He asked, "How is he?" I told him Stieg was gone, that we could see him, if he wanted, and that I'd waited for him. "When you're ready, we'll go see him," I added. We took a moment to pull ourselves together. The nurse asked me if I wanted her with us, and I said yes. (No one knew how I would react; they'd simply arranged that I might be admitted to the psychiatric ward if I broke down completely.) Erland and I went into the room where Stieg was, while the nurse remained discreetly by the door. I sat down next to Stieg and took his hand. He seemed peaceful. Sleeping, perhaps? He really did seem to be asleep. I held his hand, stroked his arm. "Stieg, dear?" I was freezing from having stayed outside so long. While he—he was still warm. You see, I told him in my thoughts, it's completely crazy, you still warm me up. Erland was sitting on the other side of Stieg, but I did not see him. At some point, he left the room. So did the nurse. I caressed Stieg's hair, his forehead, his cheeks . . . exactly the way I did when I had to awaken him from a deep sleep. As he gradually grew cold, I warmed up. I still couldn't take it in. I imagined that he was going to open one eye and start raising a ruckus, the way he always did. I remember murmuring to him, "Dearest, my love, thank you for the life you gave me, thank you for everything you've done." And I kept kissing his mouth and stroking his hair. Now he was icy cold. I stood up, completely drained, and before I left I looked at him again. He was sleeping. It was incomprehensible.

LATER OUR friends told me what had happened. Stieg had had an afternoon appointment at *Expo*, and he'd arrived at the building that morning with Jim, a friend of ours whom we'd met in Grenada in 1984. Before they went up to the *Expo* office, Jim noticed that Stieg seemed ill and unsteady on his feet. When Jim insisted that they should go to a hospital right away, Stieg refused because he wanted to go to the office first. Since the elevator was broken, he climbed up all seven floors only to collapse in a chair when he arrived. When Per and Monika, the accountant, noticed that his face was bathed in sweat and his breathing was labored, Stieg admitted that he felt a pain in his belly. An ambulance then took him and Per to a hospital only a few blocks away. Monika followed them with Stieg's jacket and backpack, which contained the *Expo* laptop computer.

A FEW weeks later, when I returned to speak with the doctor and the nurse, I learned that the health care team had been very affected by Stieg's death. They had rarely seen someone die so quickly that his wife couldn't get there in time. And they'd never seen so many people rush to the hospital, either. The nurse told me about Stieg's last moments. Shortly after he arrived at the hospital, he regained consciousness long enough to say, "You must contact Eva Gabrielsson," and give my cell phone number. Then he lost consciousness again. Forever.

THAT EVENING, Eleanor dropped Erland and me off at the apartment. Everything there seemed uncanny. Half of Stieg's last meal was still sitting on the table: a dried-up hot dog and a chocolate drink bought at the newsstand. Erland didn't want to go to bed; he kept repeating that it wasn't normal, that children shouldn't go before their parents. He was also talking about the death notice that would have to be written, trying to think which papers might report Stieg's death, and wondering who would come to the funeral. He was in shock, too. It was unbearable. Fortunately, Eleanor called with an offer to come stay the night at the apartment, which I accepted with relief. Erland slept in Stieg's office, Eleanor took the living room settee, and I was in our bedroom. The bed was still unmade.

Wednesday, November 10

AT 7:00 a.m., my sister Britt arrived from Gothenburg on the first train. Erland was pacing in the living room, composing and recomposing a death notice aloud, constantly asking us what sounded best. I was rigid: silent, staring, I felt ready to explode. Realizing that she had to get Erland out of there, Britt set off with him to walk to *Expo*, taking with her Stieg's backpack and computer, which I'd brought home from the hospital the night before. The backpack also contained Stieg's agenda, desperately needed at that day's editorial meeting at the magazine.

All afternoon, the phone and doorbell kept ringing as people called and dropped by, bringing flowers. The apartment filled up with so many bouquets that their perfume grew cloying, oppressive, and I felt as if I were in a cemetery. Friends gathered around the large table in the living room, where coffee, fruit, and cakes were laid out. Now and then someone would persuade me to take a sip or swallow a bite of something. . . . I was like a robot.

The crowd talked in hushed voices and spoke gently to me. They were there, and I was grateful. One dear friend arrived with a crate full of food, and after collapsing into my arms, she said the most levelheaded thing I would hear all day: "Thank God he died that way and wasn't murdered like you always feared. Just think how terrible it would have been, on top of everything, to have to hate someone all the rest of your life!" And that was true.

When Erland returned with Britt, he was surprised to see so many people. Not knowing anyone, he stayed on the sidelines, and that evening he went home to Umeå. Joakim, Stieg's brother, did not call me.

◻

THE PREVIOUS evening, while I'd been waiting for Erland out in front of the hospital as the gang from *Expo* was gathering, I'd heard Richard say, "It's all over now, *Expo*'s finished!" *Expo* finished? So Stieg had fought for years for nothing? *Expo* just couldn't disappear as well. No way. I was bewildered, desperate. Richard was Stieg's immediate successor: if he backed out, everything would fall apart. I phoned Mikael Ekman, a good friend and one of the stalwarts of *Expo*.

"Richard seems to be giving up. That's not an option. *Expo* mustn't fold. Or Stieg will have worked himself to death for nothing! You have to do something."

"I'll be there tomorrow."

◻

SO *EXPO* revved up again on the afternoon of November 10 with a historic meeting. Everyone who had collaborated at any time on the magazine, even just once, showed up spontaneously. There was such a crowd that they ran out of chairs, so people were standing and leaning all along the walls. Mikael ran the meeting, standing in the center of it all to relay the information from Stieg's agenda: the dates for future meetings and lectures, the deadlines for the various articles. Monika sat in a chair next to Mikael with a box of paper tissues on her lap, passing them up to him as needed because as he talked, tears kept streaming down his cheeks. Then everyone found a spot somewhere in the office to set up; some people were crying, but they all got to work.

That evening, Mikael stopped by the apartment to see Britt and me and told us simply, "It went well." We drank wine and whisky until three thirty in the morning. We couldn't manage to talk about Stieg's death, but thanks to the alcohol, at least we managed to talk to one another.

I was relieved that *Expo* would keep going. Beyond that, I felt numb.

IN SWEDEN, funerals take place a few weeks after a death. For Stieg's service we had to wait even longer because people wanted to come from all over: England, Germany, the United States. . . . I chose December 10, the day the Nobel Prizes were being handed out. That way, it would be easier to keep a low profile for the funeral in case any extremists wanted to grab some attention.

The Aftermath

RUNNING AWAY from reality, I focused on something outside myself: what was happening at *Expo*. I wanted to do whatever I could to keep the magazine going. I'm talking not about money, but about morale, because everyone was so shaken by our loss that, more than anything else, I feared they would lose heart. When I discussed this with a friend in the police force, she agreed with me, and told me how to contact the therapist they usually turned to for help with victims of traumatic stress. Later, when the *Expo* staff turned down that offer of help, I spoke with each of them individually to make sure that nobody needed anything or anyone. That evening, for the first time in a long while, I slept for seven hours straight.

I was an animal acting on instinct—a protective measure that kept anyone harmful to me at a distance. I went through life like a zombie. Every morning I woke up in tears, although my nights were dreamless. Absolute darkness. The animal in me was restless and kept me constantly in motion. I did a lot of walking, but never alone, because I no longer dared go out on my own. Not recognizing the woman I'd become, I had no idea what she might be capable of doing, to myself or to people I might meet. Like a hunted beast, I fed only on little things picked up in passing: dates, nuts, fruit.

In the days that followed, Svante Weyler came to the apartment as a representative of Norstedts to offer condolences. When he asked if I was Stieg's heir and if the books could be published as planned, I told him that of course the books should come out. And that Stieg and I had lived together as life companions.

Six days after Stieg died, Britt went home to Gothenburg. I then left my bed and started sleeping on the soft, upholstered couch so I could keep an eye on the front door and hallway, like a beast at bay. From then on I made sure I was alone. I wanted to get a grip, become myself again, without being constantly distracted by visitors. I'd spend the whole day lying down, without sleeping, under several blankets and a comforter because I was always cold. I didn't take any medications or sleeping pills. I did not have any and did not want any.

☐

NOVEMBER 17 is my birthday. It's also the day I found Stieg's gravesite. Back in the city, I had coffee with a woman friend, and for the first time I cried. Sheer relief. Finally, I'd found the right place. To my own astonishment, I said, "I can live with it." Yes, I said that, of all things. . . . In the afternoon I had an appointment with the social worker at St. Göran's Hospital and asked her about ways of helping the *Expo* team get through this first trauma. I was given to understand that too much help would be a hindrance, because they had to find their strength within themselves, as I was discovering on my own. That evening, two friends dropped by for my birthday, bringing a nice meal and some good wine. That night, though, I felt like a run-over animal that longs only for an end to its suffering.

The next morning I woke up at around seven, weeping. I ate a little porridge, a habit I'd picked up after my sister had gone home. In the evenings, I would fix myself some supper, then prove unable to eat it. But that afternoon I finally went to a doctor, who ordered a medical leave of absence for me. On the prescription he wrote, "Serious shock; two months' time off from work." Having no idea what state I was in and thinking he was exaggerating, I refused the medications he wanted me to take.

Later that afternoon, at *Expo*, I spoke with the ten-person team that regularly worked with us. They still didn't want to see the therapist I'd mentioned to them, and said they all had someone close to them to see them through.

◉

AS THE days went by, I tried to take care of our outstanding bills at home but couldn't do the math in my head, the way I always did, and I needed a calculator. When I looked at the numbers, they jumped around, wouldn't stay still. The "animal me" clearly didn't need to know how to count!

I also attempted to read Carl Laurin's essay on Carl Larsson, the illustrator and painter who was a beloved figure in the Swedish Arts and Crafts movement. All I could do, though, was trail after the letters as they went by, and I kept having to start sentences over again, trying to understand what I'd just read. At the end of the fifth page, I just quit. The animal didn't want to read, either. Would I ever be able to go back to work again?

◙

SVANTE WEYLER phoned me on November 26 and suggested during our conversation that the legal department at Norstedts should look into the inheritance situation, since they were the ones in the best position to do so. "The important thing is to arrive at a morally acceptable solution," I told him. On Wednesday, December 1, Eva Gedin, an editor with Norstedts, called to tell me that Stieg's book was fantastic, that they were considering several designs for the cover, and she invited me to come have a look at them. She added that they'd felt Stieg had grown quite close to them even though they knew almost nothing about him, and I said I hoped the memorial service, commemoration, and following reception would offer a full appreciation of Stieg's life.

Goodbyes

December 10, 2004

I WOKE up very early that morning. When I try to remember that day and the ones that followed, I can find only scraps of memories lost in a fog. I wrote nothing down in my diary; it was as if I hadn't been there. The burial service in a small chapel was only for relatives and close friends, whereas the commemoration was a more formal, public event.

It was a lovely December day, sunny, without any snow. The breeze was gentle and mild. Police were discreetly stationed everywhere. In Sweden, the law requires that the dates and hours of funerals be made available to the public online. We were afraid that right-wing extremists might disrupt the ceremony, so the funeral director and the *Expo* staff did their best to provide adequate security.

Erland flew in with his companion, and Joakim came with his wife Maj and their two children. When they saw the fifty or so guests at the chapel service they were astonished, having thought that only people close to Stieg and me would attend. I explained that they were right— that everyone there was a close friend, and that a great many of our friends were even missing because not all of them could come, especially not from abroad.

The commemoration would be held in central Stockholm at the headquarters of the Workers' Educational Association. I'd chosen eighteen speakers who would talk about Stieg, including Graeme Atkinson from *Searchlight* and Mikael Ekman from *Expo*.

Since I was supposed to speak as well, I'd tried to write out a little speech the day before, but the words hadn't come. Yet I had to say *something*. So I'd decided to show how tender and affectionate Stieg was by reading the letter he'd written me in 1977 from his hospital bed in Addis Ababa, where he had almost died. He'd told me how much he loved me and that when he returned, he wanted us to build a new life together. *But I couldn't find that letter.* I spent the entire afternoon searching the whole apartment, until late that evening, after going through every closet, I found a big cardboard box in one of our storerooms, and inside it was a small box crammed full of letters. On one manila envelope was written, "To be opened only after my death. Stieg Larsson."

The envelope contained two letters dated February 9, 1977, when Stieg was twenty-two, in Stockholm en route to Africa. This may seem difficult to believe, but I really had never seen this envelope before. Stieg had left it with his belongings at the house of the friend with whom he'd stayed in Stockholm, before his departure. Ever since then, the box had tagged along with us on all of our moves, and Stieg had probably forgotten about it.

My finding the envelope this way was so extraordinary that I looked up to heaven and said *Thank you* to Stieg. I do not believe in a life after death, but do feel there is a spiritual dimension to some things that happen. When two people have lived together for so long, each one becomes a part of the other. Sometimes I imagine Stieg relaxing in my heart, in a hammock, smiling and giving me a little wave. And we've never *had* a hammock! But that's how I see him now, lazy and carefree at last.

◻

THE FIRST letter, labeled "Will," was meant for his parents. He asked them to leave me all of his possessions and his personal writings, plus everything that had to do with politics. His science fiction books, however, were to be given to my brother. Stieg had signed his will, but without witnesses. The second letter was addressed to me.

I read some passages from it during the commemoration.

Stockholm, February 9, 1977

Eva, my love,

It's over. One way or another, everything comes to an end. It's all over some day. That's perhaps one of the most fascinating truths we know about the entire universe. The stars die, the galaxies die, the planets die. And people die too. I've never been a believer, but the day I became interested in astronomy, I think I put aside all that was left of my fear of death. I'd realized that in comparison to the universe, a human being, a single human being, me . . . is infinitely small. Well, I'm not writing this letter to deliver a profound religious or philosophical lecture. I'm writing it to tell you "farewell." I was just talking to you on the phone. I can still hear the sound of your voice. I imagine you, before my eyes . . . a beautiful image, a lovely memory I will keep until the end. At this very moment, reading this letter, you know that I am dead.

There are things I want you to know. As I leave for Africa, I'm aware of what's waiting for me. I even have the feeling that this trip could bring about my death, but it's something that I have to experience, in spite of everything. I wasn't born to sit in an armchair. I'm not like that. Correction: I wasn't like that . . . I'm not going to Africa just as a journalist, I'm going above all on a political mission, and that's why I think this trip might lead to my death.

This is the first time I've written to you knowing exactly what to say: I love you, I love you, love you, love you. I want you to know that. I want you to know that I love you more than I've ever loved anyone. I want you to know I mean that seriously. I want you to remember me but not grieve for me. If I truly mean something to you, and I know that I do, you will probably suffer when you learn I am dead. But if I really mean something to you, don't suffer, I don't want that. Don't forget me, but go on living. Live your life. Pain will fade with time, even if that's hard to imagine right now. Live in peace, my dearest love; live, love, hate, and keep fighting. . . .

I had a lot of faults, I know, but some good qualities as well, I hope. But you, Eva, you inspired such love in me that I was never able to express it to you. . . .

Straighten up, square your shoulders, hold your head high. Okay? Take care of yourself, Eva. Go have a cup of coffee. It's over. Thank you for the beautiful times we had. You made me very happy. Adieu.

I kiss you goodbye, Eva.

From Stieg, with love.

I still don't know how I managed to read his letter in front of all those people. I never looked up at anyone, but later I was told that many in the audience wept as they listened.

AFTER THE commemoration, at around five o'clock, I went home to prepare some soup so that Stieg's family and mine could gather quietly for a moment after that dark day. The Larssons stayed at the hall awhile to have coffee with all of our friends and colleagues from *Expo*. Later, at the apartment, Joakim reproached me for having refused to let Norstedts pay for the ceremony, but I disagreed: Stieg was my partner, so it was up to me to handle things. That evening was the second and last time Joakim was ever in our home.

Having spent all his early childhood with his maternal grandparents, Stieg had inherited some of their possessions, but his brother Joakim had no mementos of them and asked for a few things to remember them by. I found a small blue wooden box with traditional painted decorations, which his grandmother had used as her sewing kit, and another box, of bronze, that had come from Korea and belonged to his grandfather. Joakim took both boxes when he and his family went home to Umeå at the end of the afternoon. Erland and Gun stayed in Stockholm to attend a gathering I'd organized for seven o'clock at the Södra Theater bar, to raise a glass and share memories of Stieg with our friends, families, and even people from Norstedts. All the while, Erland kept saying that he didn't want any part of Stieg's estate.

A FEW days later, Stieg was buried. Our friends were there.

On the morning of December 22, I took an important step. I had a black ceramic burial urn, modeled on a Viking artifact and made on the island of Gotland by a professional potter, Eva-Marie Kothe, and into it I placed all that I had lost: our love, our affection, and our dreams.

A snapshot in which, lying on a rock, Stieg gazes at me, smiling. Another one, taken in Önnesmark in front of a cabin, up in Västerbotten: he's gently cradling against his chest a baby hare found in the rhubarb patch. (He loved animals, especially baby ones.) And another picture, the most beautiful one and my favorite: handsome, tanned, seductive, he's looking at me through the camera lens, cigarette in hand, at ease, as if waiting for something. Finally, a portrait in which, leaning backward, he squints into the sunlight. I also added the sketch of our cabin we'd prepared during that last summer. The final sketch, and the best one, which he'd asked to look at just once more before I sent it off to the factory that specialized in green construction. He'd pulled up a chair, sat down next to me, and we'd had fun imagining how we were going to furnish our "little writing cottage." He was transformed: warm, tender, relaxed, happy about this new future that promised to be more intimate and serene. He'd come back to me as he used to be, and for me, it was like falling in love all over again.

Then I added to that black urn some phone numbers of rooms for rent in the archipelago that I'd written down so he could take a week's vacation and keep working, without being bothered, on the fourth volume of the *Millennium* saga or correcting the proofs of the first three. I would often find him chuckling to himself on the living room settee: "You'll never guess what Lisbeth is cooking up!" Then he'd start writing, adjusting some detail he'd asked me to check in my documentation files.

I placed the ceramic vessel full of our lives on a shelf. And behind it I slipped a few sheets of handmade paper I'd bought at Kvarnbyn in Mölndal, outside Gothenburg. On a blue sheet I'd written down what I had lost, and on a yellow one, what I wanted now: "To survive another year."

The Vengeance of the Gods

IN *THE Millennium Trilogy*, Lisbeth Salander marks her body with tattoos as a reminder of all those who have hurt her and on whom she wishes to take revenge. In my case, such people are etched into my memory.

Several weeks after Stieg's passing, I still couldn't manage to find words, even in my thoughts, to express the rage I felt toward this death that was so unfair—and toward those who, directly or indirectly, consciously or unconsciously, had helped it along.

Stieg and I had dreamed about changing the world, become actively involved in our causes, sacrificed so much for our battles—and now I was left with a sense of tremendous failure.

I thought back over all those years of frustration that had

wounded the man of my life, years during which some people had refused to recognize his abilities, his immense store of knowledge, and his worth. Time after time I'd watched his disappointment at not having been accepted as a journalist at TT, his pain over so many hopes that were dashed and all those promises he'd believed in only to see them broken in the end. I relived his anguish, discouragement, and his constant fear, after he'd left TT, that *Expo* would go under in spite of all his efforts every month to find funding for it. I remembered him coming home so late in the evenings, worn out, sleeping more and more badly, fitfully. I recalled a terrible period when too much stress brought on a painful, chronic gum inflammation, for which a doctor had prescribed very strong medications. Feeling pressured from all directions, Stieg talked to me about his problems, of course, seeking advice, but he had to make all of his own decisions. Overwhelmed by this horrible flood of black memories, I was in despair. I could not cope with it.

Then, sensing that I might find a way to grapple with my depression, I turned to mythology for a violent, raw, unflinching way to express all this, something that would measure up to my suffering. We had many books on the subject, and I found what I was looking for in the *Elder Edda*—a collection of poems in Old Norse, the ancestor of the modern Scandinavian languages—and in particular in the *Hávamál* (*Sayings of the High One* or *The Words of the Most-High*). I realized that my catharsis would pass through the writing of a *nið* (pronounced *nee*), a traditional curse, which I would recite during a magic ceremony.

I set the date: December 31.

In Scandinavian mythology, the *nið*, written in Skaldic poetry (perhaps the most complex verse form ever created in the West), is a kind of taunting curse hurled at one's enemies. It was read or carved in the runic alphabet on a stake of hazelwood known as "the staff of infamy," which was driven into the ground. A horse was sacrificed and its head stuck on top of the stake, turned toward the poet's mortal enemy. Although its origins are lost to time, this rite crops up even until about the tenth century in the Icelandic sagas. And in the 1980s, Icelanders are said to have used it against the occupants of the NATO military base at the Keflavik International Airport, built by the United States during World War II. Iceland joined NATO in 1949, and Americans returned there in force in 1951. They must have been nonplussed to wake up one morning and find the grinning, blood-streaked head of a horse stuck on a stake, its mane blowing in the wind! They didn't leave until 2006, but if the ceremony really did take place, I'm sure it did some good—at least for those who carried it out.

On December 31, 2004, Britt and I took a walk along the Montelius cliff path, toward Slussen (the Lock), which connects Gamla Stan with Södermalm. Before returning to the apartment on the small island of Reimersholm, just west of Södermalm, we bought wine and a leg of lamb. For more than a hundred years, a distillery on Reimersholm has produced spirits to make aquavit, the most popular Swedish drink. Aquavit is essentially vodka flavored with spices and berries, and today "Reimersholm" has become the generic name for the eighteen or so varieties of aquavit.

When Mikael Blomqvist drinks Reimersholm aquavit in the trilogy, Stieg is of course toasting "our" little island.

While the garlic-and-cinnamon-studded leg of lamb was cooking, I went off alone to finish my *nið*. I was nervous, because I needed to get it done in time—but I wanted it to be perfect, too. To help me out, Britt had called one of her friends, an Icelandic scholar, to ask her if there were any precise rules for the writing of a *nið*. After a moment of silence at the other end of the phone, her friend had asked, "You really mean *nið*, in the sense of an insulting rant?"

"That's it."

"Okay, you're in luck. My family's here, I'll ask them."

When she came back to the phone she told Britt that as far as they all knew, there were no particular rules about the rhyme scheme or number of syllables. On the other hand, she pointed out, there was a distinct obligation to limit the curse to the time it took for the foe to change his attitude and actions and formally recognize his faults.

Relieved, I was able to get to work, and made sure that I cursed Stieg's enemies only until they realized what they had done.

The *nið* was ready at eight that evening, just before the guests arrived, the last of whom didn't show up until ten and in evening dress, having slipped away from a fancy New Year's Eve party. Half an hour later, we left the apartment and headed west to the farthest spit of Reimersholm, which juts out into Lake Mälaren. The temperature hadn't gone below zero, so it wasn't very cold and the lake hadn't frozen over. There was hardly any snow, and wherever New Year's Eve parties were in full swing, windows shone brightly in the dark night. At the end of the island, I leaned back against a wooden barrier, with my back to the water. Behind me, on the other shore of the lake, were Eleanor's house and the dock where I used to tie up the communal rowboat I borrowed whenever I went over to see her. In front of me stood the tree under which Stieg and I had often sat at night with a thermos of hot coffee, and the hill where we used to picnic in the summer. Happy memories were streaming by . . . it was a peaceful moment, moving and serene.

One of the guests produced some large candles from his backpack and set them alight on top of the wooden barrier. Then, to my great surprise, he pulled out a torch that he lighted and held aloft. With this fire, the pagan ritual was in its element! All of our friends there knew as well as I did what this ceremony was for. Speaking slowly and very distinctly, I read the *nið* I had composed. And I succeeded at last in expressing what I felt.

> *I am reading a* nið *for Stieg*
> *I am reading a* nið *for you who were against him*
> *You who took his time, his knowledge, and his friendship*
> *Giving nothing in return*
> *Friends are duty-bound to be loyal lifelong to their friends*
> *And to render gift for gift*
> *Friends reply with mockery to the mockery of others*
> *And to lies with lies*
> (Hávamál 42)

Friends are duty-bound to be loyal lifelong to their friends
And loyal as well to any friend of their friends
But no one should befriend
A friend's enemy
(Hávamál 43)

This nið *is for you:*
Evil, sly, cowardly
You who think yourselves above others
You who lead them to misfortune and death

You the evil ones who wished to rob Stieg of life
You who plotted, spied, and stirred up prejudice
You above all, N. N.

You the sly
You who let Stieg work himself to pieces
For your own profit and your career alone
You above all, N. N.

You the cowardly
You who let Stieg fight your battles
While you raked in the salaries of your cushy jobs
You, too many to mention

All sorts of you
In suits, ties, and wingtips
This nið *is for you*

I hope
That the trickster Loki spellbinds your eyes
So you will see only enemies around you forevermore
And you will all cut one another down

That hammer-wielding Thor will shatter your strength
When you indulge in violence
Against the true soul-friends of Stieg

That Lord Odin and our three Fates—Urd, Skuld, Verdandi
Strike you with confusion
Sinking your careers and ill-gotten gains

That Freyr and Freyja—fertility, fruitfulness, and love
And light-bearing Baldr strip away your joy in life
Turning bread, beer, and desire
Into stones, muddy water, and dejection

That one-eyed Odin sends Hugin and Munin
Twin ravens of thought and memory
To peck open your minds so that good common sense
Can drive out your ignorance

To peck at your eyes
To make you see what you do
So you cannot remain blind forever

To peck at your hearts
Making what your meanness and stupidity have wrought
Haunt you with the same anxieties and terrors
That afflict your victims

Until you learn, see, and feel
Until you change
This nið *will last and linger*

I sacrifice this horse in Lake Mälaren
So that this nið *may course upstream through fresh water*
And downstream to the sea
To reach all the lands of the earth
And all evil, sly, and cowardly souls

And so that the horse I offer
May give renewed power to the nið
In the spring thaw, the summer rains,
The hail of autumn, and the winter snows
To pour down on you year in and out
To find you, wherever you may hide

N. N.? THESE initials don't correspond to the real names of those for whom this *nið* is meant. There's no point in trying to find out who they are. But *they* will recognize themselves. And so does everyone who contributed to Stieg's deadly exhaustion.

A thousand years ago, at this stage of the ceremony, a horse was beheaded with a sword in sacrifice. To the Vikings of those days, this animal was sacred: their friend, companion, and the precious guarantor of their happiness and survival.

In 1987, at a job where I was a foreman and things were quite difficult to manage, a workman, a potter in his spare time, gave me one of his creations to thank me for my efforts with the team. It was two ceramic horses that had fused together in the heat of the kiln. I was particularly fond of this present, which to me symbolized absolute beauty, a job well done, recognition of my work, and the spirit of fraternity. With a sharp blow I separated the two animals, and turning toward the water, I threw one of them into this lake once sailed by Vikings.

In the silence that followed, we gazed for a long time at the place where the horse had vanished, relieved to have heard spoken aloud what we had all been thinking to ourselves. Then we hugged and kissed, vowing always to look after one another. In the darkness, I slipped off to our place to fetch some glasses and single malt Scotch. When I returned, I poured a small libation into the lake before serving my friends. Barley, from which this whisky is made, is also fed to horses, so I symbolically gave strength to my horse to speed him on his mission of revenge. And also assured, according to mythology, that the *nið* itself would be protected.

By now it was almost eleven thirty. In Sweden, fireworks go off everywhere at midnight on New Year's Eve, and people pour out into the streets: it's a wonderfully joyous moment. My friends and I had a drink together, and fifteen minutes later, right before crowds of revelers arrived, we went back to my apartment to continue our special evening. I brought the second horse home with me from the lake and will keep him, even though he cannot stand up anymore on his own.

I felt free and at peace. My ceremony was my therapy, just as *The Millennium Trilogy* was for Stieg. Now I could envisage going on living without him.

My 2005 Diary

KEEPING A diary helped anchor me in reality. I filled pages and pages, sometimes even noting down what I was having for breakfast! Looking back on it, I think the diary was a way of proving to myself that I was alive. I've selected only important dates here, so that the reader may discover what I learned—to my astonishment—as the months went by.

◉

Thursday, January 13, 2005
MEETING AT Norstedts, ten o'clock. The publishing house asked some legal experts what my position could be regarding the management of Stieg's work. After review-

ing their report, I point out that it never mentions the company Stieg discussed with me. What a shock! I find out that the company was never even started! Appalled, I repeat what Stieg explained to me: there's no point in signing a "domestic partner" contract, as we were thinking of doing in March 2004, because the two of us would be the co-owners of that company. But Svante Weyler simply tries to tell me that the novels have been sold in Norway, that negotiations are under way with the Netherlands. . . . I don't want to hear about *their* business negotiations! I'm devastated. How could Stieg have been so naïve?

Weyler promises to get in touch with my lawyer, Malin (who is busy drawing up the inventory of Stieg's assets), as well as with Stieg's father and brother, Erland and Joakim, to find a solution. I think: God only knows what's going to happen now!

When I get home, I send an email to Joakim telling him everything. He replies that there must certainly be some way to carry out Stieg's wishes and set up the company, even after the fact.

◼

Saturday, January 15

MESSAGE FROM Joakim on the answering machine. I call him back to tell him in detail about the shock I got at the Thursday meeting when I learned that nothing had been done, which meant that I didn't exist. Joakim feels it should be enough to tell Weyler that an oral agreement existed with Stieg that everything should come to me. And he adds that Weyler phoned Erland, who'd been unable to explain what was said. Then that evening, Erland calls me to say he agrees with me about having the chairman of *Expo*, Per-Erik Nilsson, handle everything, especially the negotiations with Norstedts.

◻

THE NEXT day, I speak with Per-Erik, who agrees to represent me. I'm greatly relieved that someone like him—a lawyer, a former judge, the former head of the Judicial Department of the Council of State under Prime Minister Olof Palme, a former chief ombudsman of Sweden—is taking charge of what I cannot handle on my own.

We meet for the first time on January 21 at the offices of *Expo*, since I've gone back to work up in Falun as of January 10, and am out of Stockholm for four days a week.

I send an email to Joakim to explain all this and let him know that Per-Erik will be contacting him and Erland. Joakim tells me to keep my chin up, saying that I'm right to entrust the handling of this business to an experienced lawyer. He tells me again that there must be some way to deal with this that effectively proceeds just as if Stieg and I had been married. He signs off by asking me to take care of myself.

In mid-February, the inventory of assets is completed. Stieg's father and brother did not come to the meeting at the lawyer's office.

▣

Tuesday, February 22

I WORKED all day long at the office, and dealt efficiently with a respectable number of files. I even spent a long time digging through the EU directives and regulations to find the rest of some information I needed.

This evening, at home, all became silent and calm. Surrounded by this silence, concentrating on myself, I began to cry. Wrenching sobs, dreadfully deep. Everything I have lost is in this suffering, along with a cruel feeling of insecurity. During the day, there's no room for silence, or sorrow: they're beaten down. In the evening, though, they rise again, stretching delicately, almost tenderly, and they take up all the room.

▣

Sunday, March 20

A FEW weeks ago, I'd made up my mind to consult a crisis therapist, but after the tsunami last December in Southeast Asia, all of the psychological assistance services offered by the county council have been devoted as a matter of priority to survivors of that tragedy. It's been five months since Stieg died, and I've only just now found a private therapist. We met for the first time today. After all those months when I couldn't manage to express my pain, suddenly I'm being asked to talk about it. I still can't do it. I could only paint a picture of what I feel like: a ball.

◉

Thursday, March 24

I'VE RECEIVED several emails from Joakim this month about inheritance taxes and accounting surpluses. He also informed me that Weyler had sent him the first volume of *The Millennium Trilogy* and asked me if I'd gotten one, too. I had no idea what he was talking about. After March 24, I never heard from Joakim again.

◉

Tuesday, March 29

AFTER EASTER weekend, I took two and a half days off because I didn't have the courage to go up to Falun for such a short time. I stayed in Stockholm to change the apartment around a bit. I wanted to clear the books out of Stieg's office, which is also the guest room, and rearrange the furniture. So his whole life passed through my hands. Sorting out his beloved books, his warmth and insatiable curiosity became tangible, and I kept stopping to cry awhile. I got back to work, but tearful despair struck again, a rolling gray sea pouring out of me. I'm sad, so infinitely sad.

◉

Tuesday, April 5

THIS AFTERNOON I sent an email to Joakim to tell him

that after calling the tax authorities to ask for an extension regarding filing the estate taxes, I'd been given until June 16. Anything longer than that would have had to be requested in writing. I also explained to Joakim that I hadn't yet dared face sorting through Stieg's papers, but that all the receipts would still have to be found.

I added that I was intending to ask for help from the guy in charge of accounting where Stieg worked, because the receipts to be used as deductions had to be separated from the ones representing expenses for which he'd already been reimbursed. Since the accountant had already helped him with his previous tax returns, he'd be familiar with the problem.

I also shared with Joakim the fact that I was seeing my therapist every two weeks, which I definitely felt was a good thing, because as he said himself, that's how you can learn to know yourself better. Which was perhaps vital right now, when I no longer much knew who I was.

I added that I wasn't very strong these days and sometimes had to stay home from work. And that I missed Stieg unspeakably, but I knew he wanted me to keep going and not give up on everything he'd begun. Easy to say, but so hard to do, after losing half of myself.

I closed by asking him to say hello to Maj for me, to take care of himself and not overwork, because he shouldn't end up like Stieg just because, like Stieg, he couldn't bring himself to say "no."

I received no reply to my email. One month later, I understood why.

◎

Monday, May 9

THIS MORNING I received a letter from the tax authorities
marked "For your information." I am thereby informed that,
regarding the inventory of Stieg's assets and the distribution
of his estate sent to them on April 14 by Joakim and Erland,
everything goes to them—including Stieg's half of our apartment. They're giving Joakim's children 100,000 kronor each
($15,000) from the advance offered by Norstedts and are leav-
ing me the furniture, valued at 1,200 kronor (less than $200)!
Then I remembered that on April 13, when I'd phoned Erland
to find out what was happening, he'd said he had no idea and
that I ought to call Joakim instead, because he was the one
taking care of everything. Erland was cold and distant. The
next day, the two of them sent the inheritors' division of the
estate off to the tax authorities.

What an insult to Stieg! To his life, to our life for thirty-
two years! I'm wracked with anger, outrage, panic, and despair. If Erland and Joakim demand Stieg's half of the
apartment from me, I couldn't afford to buy it from them.
Where will I go?

Before taking the train to Falun, I called Per-Erik
Nilsson to tell him about this infamous "For your information." So far, he hadn't done a thing for me! But he
promised me he would now intervene on my behalf.

◎

Saturday, May 14

I PHONE Svante Weyler to let him know that while filing some papers, I'd finally found the original contract Stieg signed, a document Weyler had been pestering me about back in December. Strangely, though, it no longer interests him at all. He even says something unbelievable to me: that the best solution would have been for Norstedts to manage Stieg's literary legacy.

▣

IN THE days that follow, my sister Britt calls me. She wants me to authorize her to speak to Erland about that letter from the tax authorities. When I won't allow her to get involved, she finally blurts out, "Eva, I know something you don't and that I didn't want to tell you earlier, because you were in no condition to hear it." On the evening of Stieg's funeral service, on December 10, 2004, someone came over to Britt to tell her, "Watch out, they've already talked about taking it all." I stand there, paralyzed, clutching my cell phone. So everything had already been decided.

Britt did try to talk to Erland. He told her that I was mentally ill. The proof? That I wanted to give money to *Expo*! "And a foundation in Stieg's memory—what do you think of that?" she asked him. Long silence. In fact, he doesn't want any money given to anyone. Conclusion: Stieg must also have been mentally ill, since he was the one who wanted *Expo* to receive some money.

When the news of these developments got around, I began receiving wonderful messages from my friends. Some of them even offered to be my guarantor so I could borrow money to buy Stieg's half of our apartment from his family. That's when I realized that at least I was rich . . . in friendship.

�

STIEG HAS been gone now for seven months. I'm barely starting to recover. Today I talked with Gruvstad, the therapist, about this deeply rooted belief I've had ever since childhood: a great happiness is always followed by a misfortune that is just as intense. She assured me that this isn't true and that I mustn't always be afraid of being punished if I feel good. I came home with a (very) tiny sensation of lightness. I took out a new lamp of yellow glass I'd bought, set it on the glossy white windowsill, and turned it on for the first time. Then I put together a whatnot, an étagère for Stieg's office, and on it I placed three pictures: the black-and-white photograph of him as a child with his grandparents, in front of their little wooden house; the photo I'd taken of the inside of their kitchen when we went back there; and a snapshot of me. I looked at Stieg and asked him to watch over me. Then I started crying again, with my head hanging, for a long time.

◙

Tuesday, June 7

THROUGH THE Föreningsbanken in Umeå, where the Larssons live, I received a bankbook representing what is left—after they'd helped themselves—of a building society account Stieg had: 1,290.63 kronor, or $181.41. What humiliation. What contempt. Aside from that bankbook, no other news from Erland or Joakim.

Friday, June 10

WENT TO Handelsbanken to take out enough from our joint account, Stieg's and mine, to pay the 8,640 kronor ($1,282) due the lawyers for their inventory of Stieg's assets. Of the 30,000 kronor that remained, I took 15,000 ($2,250) without informing the estate. I couldn't care less. I don't want to have anything more do to with the Larssons.

What I'd like to see passed is a legislative amendment to the law on concubinage. I don't want other people to suffer the same injustice I did! I called Ronny Olander, a Swedish MP in the Social Democratic Party, and Gustav Fridolin, a Green Party MP. The latter was so shaken by my story that he asked me to send him an email right away with full details.

Saturday, June 11

WHILE GETTING ready to refinish the floor in Stieg's office, I carried piles of papers into the living room, and so came across some documents from the Ikano Bank. I'd completely forgotten that I'd transferred Stieg's life insurance policy there. Now I can get money to pay for the trip from Falun to Stockholm to attend the first executive meeting of *Expo*'s new board next Thursday. For travel during the day, the ticket costs more, going from 26 to 69 euros (from $34 to $91). I didn't have enough in my account and won't get my next paycheck for two weeks.

❒

THE REFINISHED floor is a disaster! I have to call the supplier of the compound used to fill in the cracks. It's really a miserable chore to make this room over, but I must do it. I can't subcontract this job. One can't farm out grief. What with shifting around all I have left of Stieg, various objects and books, he's everywhere in the apartment. And that reminds me of all the things he was interested in, all he did, all he cared about so passionately. . . . It moves me and upsets me, and it hurts.

❒

Saturday, July 2

I REDID the floor. I've wept nonstop over these few square feet of wood, the tears trickling down between the floorboards on which I knelt, slaving away. What a hell. But why didn't I do this when Stieg was alive? He would have been so happy to have the floor looking nice. I do have to make over this room now, though, to have a place where I can finish my book on Hallman and organize the Stieg Larsson Foundation I hope to create. And for that I'll need to be able to hang on to the apartment! The constant anguish I live in is just awful. Per-Erik Nilsson made an offer to the Larssons and to Svante Weyler at Norstedts: that I should manage Stieg's literary estate. And he raised the question of the apartment. Deafening silence. Since March, nothing from the Larssons, nothing from Norstedts.

◙

DURING JULY, I learn that a *Millennium* audiobook edition is due to come out. I remember Weyler mentioning this in December 2004. But there was no contract for audiobooks between Stieg and Norstedts. . . .

◙

Wednesday, July 20

FIRST WEEK of vacation. I've learned that an offer for the

film rights of the trilogy from Strix, a Swedish television production company with major dealings in the Nordic countries, has been rejected by Norstedts, which wants a bigger suitor. I took another look at the contract Norstedts has for Stieg's crime novels to see if they really control those rights. And no, they don't. There's nothing there about any audiobooks, either. After talking with friends and colleagues in publishing, Stieg had in fact decided not to let Norstedts be the agent for film rights to his work. If a film adaptation of the trilogy became a possibility, he wanted to make any decisions about that two or three years down the line, after the first book had come out, meaning in around 2007–2008. Stieg intended to find an agent and a production company in the United States, to make sure any film would be a top-quality product. So in that contract Stieg signed in April 2004, he didn't check off the box for film rights. What's more, strangely enough, outside of the separate agreement giving the Pan Agency (the Norstedts foreign rights department) the right to sell the novels abroad, the main contract deals only with a paperback edition.

Puzzling over this oddity, I found an explanation: when it was time to sign the contracts, the two separate documents were presented to Stieg for his signature, but no one realized that the second one was actually *both* contracts, stapled together by mistake. The first document concerned the paperback rights, and Stieg signed the last page, so that contract is valid. When he signed the last page of the second document, which was supposed to be the main publishing contract, he was really signing only the Pan Agency contract again. So Stieg never signed the principal contract. Stieg and I never noticed, and neither did Norstedts.

I could imagine what happened then. After Stieg's death, when Norstedts discovered the problem, they had Erland and Joakim sign a new contract so that they'd have a free hand and could get the books out quickly. Further contracts must have been signed later to allow the publisher to sell the film rights. All supposition, of course. Anyway, no one who knows Stieg would believe that he'd let his family or publisher control his work or his image. That's completely absurd—he was way too independent for that! Which is why it's so important to me to obtain contol of the intellectual property rights to all his work. I'm thinking above all of his articles for *Expo*, for *Searchlight*, his books on the far right, and so forth.

◧

I'VE FINISHED packing for my second week of vacation. Tomorrow I take off into the archipelago. I'm supplied with half a pound of Lipton tea, some mustard, tomato pasta, couscous, salt and pepper, oil, vinegar, and dishwashing liquid, which I've put into little jars from my pantry.

Plus my Koala Macintosh and a pad of paper in a leatherette folder. I have of course hooked the compass and survival knife onto my Klättermusen jacket. And slipped the can of mace into a pocket.

◉

Thursday, August 4

A PERVASIVE melancholy came over me on July 19 during my first week of vacation without Stieg, and I can't escape it anymore. It's everywhere. I see it in the summer evening light as orange melts into gold, ocher, and copper. The life I knew is over. The one I used to imagine will never be. I'd like all this to end quickly. Rather than wait for nothing in particular. . . .

◉

Wednesday, August 10

PER-ERIK NILSSON phoned to ask me if I'd read his agreement proposal. He says he did his best to look after my interests. "You're sure that your chief concern is control of the intellectual property, and not the money?" Yes, I assured him, once again.

◉

Friday, August 12

TOWARD THE end of the day, Svante Weyler finally answered my question about the film rights: Erland and Joakim did in fact sign a contract with Norstedts. Absolutely infuriated, I left a message for Per-Erik Nilsson to let him know that contrary to what he'd been told at

Norstedts, the contract had definitely been signed.

◉

A FEW days later, I would read an article in the *Sydsvenska Dagbladet* announcing that *The Millennium Trilogy* would soon be adapted for film by the Swedish film company Yellow Bird.

◉

Tuesday, August 16

I FINALLY called Joakim to find out about the apartment. He suggested something that was simply beyond belief, saying the problem would be solved if we were to use the apartment jointly . . . but that this certainly wouldn't interest me!

Only then did he tell me they were finally going to give me their half of the apartment—and added that he was so fed up with handling all of Stieg's paperwork that I would have to cope with the red tape involved. Do I dare believe him?

◉

DURING THE following week I went with Britt to see our old neighbors in Önnesmark, where we grew up, not far from Umeå. We wanted to see Stieg's father and brother, but every time Britt called them, they said they were too busy. We were finally able to meet with them in a restaurant in town. They kept sticking to small talk, so after an hour of that I bluntly announced that we had something to discuss: the best way to manage Stieg's work. After a moment's thought, Joakim explained that they were afraid that if I had control of the intellectual property, this might be in conflict with the film company's rights to develop the characters in *The Millennium Trilogy*. No matter what Britt and I brought up, he kept replying that he would have to talk first with Svante Weyler. Then he reaffirmed their decision to give me their half of the apartment, but repeated that I would have to take care of the formalities.

As we were saying goodbye near the bus stop, Erland began to explain to me that the problem lay in the fact that I might get married someday, which posed a risk for them. "Stieg was the one I wanted to marry," I replied. Then Joakim suggested that I marry Erland, which would solve all of the problems concerning the division of the estate. I just *froze* . . . and Britt stared at him in horror. Of course, he added, this marriage would only be on paper!

Tuesday, August 23

AN EMAIL from Svante Weyler. Ole Søndberg, a producer at Yellow Bird, which bought the *Millennium* film rights, would like to meet me. They're about to begin writing the screenplay and are eagerly seeking any information that might help them. Weyler also said that the reviews of Stieg's first book are fantastic, that he couldn't imagine a better début.

So from now on, I know:

Joakim is a double-dealer, acting in bad faith.

Erland is supporting him, because Joakim—not Stieg—is the son he always considered his.

Consequences:

Permanently break off relations with Erland and Joakim.

Do as Stieg said: "Avenge your friends."

Seek help from other people.

▣

Friday, September 9

I'VE HIRED Erica Striby, of the Bergquist Law Firm, to draw up the deed of gift for their half of the apartment, which she sent off to the Larssons today.

▣

Tuesday, September 13

SVANTE WEYLER is leaving the position of editorial director at Norstedts. Eva Gedin, Stieg's editor, will replace him. No news from the Larssons.

It's been ten months since Stieg died. Neither his father nor his brother has asked me where he was buried.

▣

IN THE days that followed, there was no reply to my lawyer's letter about deeding over the other half of the apartment. If Stieg knew that his publisher wanted, against his wishes, to make a film from his books, he would be furious and react violently to this betrayal. But if he saw what his father and brother are doing to me, he would be wounded beyond all measure and would not quit until he'd had his revenge. Attacking me would have been an attack on him.

▣

Friday, October 7

MEETING WITH the Yellow Bird people at the Pan Agency office.

The screenwriter, Lars Björkman, starts off with a direct question: "Have you read the fourth volume?"

Reply: "No!"

And voilà—one less question!

A few minutes later, another question: "Stieg must have done a lot of research. Where is his documentation?"

"Would you like to take a look?" I then bring out a whole pile of Stieg's writing I've brought with me: his books on the far right, his last article for *Searchlight*, his reports for CRIDA (*Centre de recherche et d'information sur la démocratie et l'autonomie*), for Tel Aviv University, for CRISP (*Centre de recherche et d'information socio-politiques*), etc.

"You'll find names, people, events, opinions, reflections," I add, while they examine the material. "This is Stieg's life, and that is all his documentation. His crime novels flow naturally from the rest of his work."

Another question settled!

There were more points raised, for example the places and addresses in the trilogy. I explained that, thanks to my profession, I had furnished them. Next, the characters. "Aside from those everyone knows," someone asked, "like the boxer Paolo Roberto, are there other real people in the novels?"

Answer: "Yes." Next question!

"And that style, that way of speaking, where does that come from?"

Here I was careful to explain that the atmosphere of these books was different from that of classic crime fiction because Stieg came from Västerbotten County, and I advised the Yellow Bird team to pay close attention to the influence of the Bible on his fictional world. One of the women there agreed with me, and to my surprise, announced that she was the daughter of Per Olov Enquist— a contemporary author I've already mentioned in a similar context, whose works reflect his roots in the isolated northern region of Västerbotten.

At the end of the meeting, we parted on good terms, and I was invited to come to Ystad, where Yellow Bird has its headquarters. As for my collaboration, that remained somewhat up in the air.

▣

Wednesday, October 19

PER-ERIK NILSSON phoned at around eight this evening to read me what Erland and Joakim's lawyer

Svanström had faxed to him from Umeå. In short:

The response to my request to take over the management of the intellectual rights to Stieg's work is NO. The Larssons will continue to handle that, in concert with Norstedts. Or someone of Norstedts' choice.

The response to the deed of gift for their half of the apartment is NO. Unless I hand the fourth manuscript for the *Millennium* series over to Norstedts. In which case, the discussion regarding intellectual property rights might also be reconsidered.

The response concerning the remainder of the outstanding loan Stieg took out to buy our home is that it should be paid for by his life insurance.

And finally, they emphasize that they "have been generous" since they're leaving me Stieg's bank accounts, the furniture, and his life insurance (of which I am in fact the beneficiary and which should not be included in his estate).

"How *mean*!" I exclaimed.

"Yes, that's about right," replied Per-Erik.

These new and unexpected arbitrary demands must be due to my lack of cooperation during the meeting with the film production company last October 7.

So everything started up again. For the umpteenth time, trapped in insomnia, I had trouble sleeping. I'd get up, smoke, go back to bed, get up again, over and over, before dropping off at dawn with barbed wire rolling around in my head. Then I stopped eating. Again. For the I-don't-know-how-manyeth time.

◉

Thursday, October 20

I SENT an email to Eva Gedin at Norstedts and to Magdalena Hedlund at the Pan Agency to inform them of Erland and Joakim's responses. I explained that since the Larssons refused to grant me the intellectual property rights, Norstedts should therefore tell Yellow Bird that it is the Larssons, not I, who must give them the information they had wanted from me. There was no reply to my email.

◉

Friday, October 21

A DISCOURAGING and exhausting meeting with Per-Erik Nilsson. Not only are we at a standstill, but he's suggesting that I "think over this business about the fourth manuscript." I blew up. "They'll never get it! It's probably in the computer that belongs to *Expo*, and the contents of that laptop are protected by the Constitution: all of Stieg's contacts, all of his informants, all of his sources for his work as a journalist must be in there! Those vital documents cannot fall into the hands of these people, *because it's none of their business!*"

Then Per-Erik had to leave to go take care of his grandchildren. I was worn out. I felt more alone than ever.

◉

Wednesday, October 26

I CAN'T think anymore, can't organize thoughts, can't work. I went to see the head of personnel, who sized up the situation. "Go home," she said, "you'll be better off there." In the train coming back to Stockholm, I watched the autumn countryside fly past. The landscape looked heavy, almost glutted. The earth was full of colors—brown, green, ocher, black—and at the same time, tired. Like me. I was so tired, but also consumed with the desire to keep fighting. For Stieg. The way *he* would do. The way he would ask me to do.

When I got home, I unplugged all the phones and decided not to read any of my emails for a few days. For the first time in a year, I was going to rest, read poetry, think things over, stroll around, go look at Lake Mälaren. My *nið* for Stieg flows in its waters. That makes me happy. Then, in the silence of our home, Stieg came back, because suddenly there was room for him. While I listened to "You Are Always on My Mind," I wept. I began to talk to Stieg. I felt terrible and useless for not having managed to protect his life's work. It was as if I had betrayed him.

◙

Monday, October 31

WOKE UP at around ten this morning and went down to the Furusundsleden, the northernmost marine channel into Stockholm, to look at the water stream by. I looked for a stone to place on Stieg's grave. What should it be like? I would certainly know it when I saw it. I did not see it in the water. I walked along, my steps taking me toward a big red rock, smooth in some places, rough and cracked in others, and streaked with black. It made me think of Stieg. Soft and tough at the same time. Solid, unshakable in its convictions. Wearing its heart on its sleeve, visible only to those who know it well. There was no way for me to break off a little piece. That's only natural, I thought: this rock, like Stieg, is too all-of-a-piece to be broken. I'm not going to worry anymore about that stone I wanted. It's there. Like him.

Later that day I went out again to walk in the forest, and as I entered the woods, the cold settled down on my shoulders. I gathered lingonberries, acid and refreshing. Some blueberries, too, but they were tasteless, frozen, and no good at all. The October sun beamed down through any yellow leaves still clinging to the trees. A lovely autumn for a sad woman. I climbed a rounded hill, walking on its mossy carpet, a soft path, but one that led nowhere.

I'll go toward the light, at least, I decided.

At the top there was nothing to see. Still, I stopped a moment in the sun and thought, I'm a little human being on a big hill, an insignificant thing in this world.

I'd failed in the one thing of any importance after Stieg died: defending him. To me, this failure was a betrayal. I didn't have the courage to go on; tears were running down my cheeks, dripping from my chin, even starting to soak through my wool coat. I kept saying, "Forgive me, forgive me. . . ."

Suddenly I heard a sound so strange I had no idea what it was. Looking up, I saw a raven: royal and nonchalant, he came closer, and began to fly over me in crescent-shaped curves. It was as if he'd gone out to do an errand and, when turning toward home, had consented to make this little detour for me, thinking, Well, all right, if it's really important. He spoke to me for a long time in a deep melodious voice. All at once, I was in the *nið* for Stieg, where I'd asked Odin's ravens, Hugin and Munin, to peck holes in the head, eyes, and heart of all the cruel, sly, and cowardly people who had made Stieg suffer.

I was so astounded that I thought the impossible, without fear or hesitation: This isn't for real. Odin, you've sent me your raven?

I do not know what the bird was saying, but its magnificent voice touched my heart, soothed my despair, and brought me peace. As if I'd been told, Everything is fine, you mustn't worry anymore. So why don't you head back home? On the way back I stumbled sometimes, thanks to my lack of sleep and appetite, but I was no longer alone. Stieg was supporting me. "You Were Always on My Mind." I know that, my beloved friend; even when you didn't have much time to spend with me, I know that I was always in your thoughts. As you are in mine.

That evening, I realized that the important thing now was not to go under. When I got home, I sent a few SMS messages to say that I was fine, that I simply needed peace, some quiet time to reflect and rest.

◙

Thursday, November 3

I CHANGED my landline and cell phone numbers. From now on, everyone except my friends and family will have to go through Per-Erik or another lawyer to reach me. I left the phone store incredibly relieved.

Then I went to see our family doctor, who was upset by my condition. I did not want any medication or a two months' leave of absence from work, but I did accept a month of part-time. I need to work, to occupy my mind. I also need to relax and live a normal life.

◙

Wednesday, November 9

TONIGHT WAS the commemoration of Kristallnacht and the first anniversary of Stieg's death. I spent half the day working on the speech I'd be giving along with the photos I had to present. I put on black pants, the lavender Linnéa Braun blouse I bought at Myrorna (a really neat Salvation Army store), and a suede jacket from the flea market in Falun. I wore my hair loose and put on a bit of makeup.

The gathering was held at Cirkeln, a restaurant, where coffee and cakes were served.

Daniel Poohl of *Expo* began his speech by saying that he didn't have any one particular memory of Stieg, but rather, a continuous memory of him . . . listening. "Stieg listened to absolutely everyone, including people we found completely uninteresting. For example, we kept telling him to stop listening to that nitpicking idiot Jan Milld, of Blågula Frågor, a small political association that focuses on immigration issues: 'You're wasting your time with him!' You know what happened: Jan Milld wound up the secretary general of the Sweden Democrats, a nationalist movement. Everyone was flabbergasted except . . . Stieg—who had listened to him! It's not surprising that many higher-ups in that party sincerely regretted Stieg's death, because *he listened to them*. He was like that, Stieg: he listened."

I was so impressed, once again, by the elegance of Daniel's intelligence and his conviction.

When it was my turn to speak, I was quite calm.

I began by recalling that Stieg and I had worked together for thirty-two years and lived together for thirty. And that people do what they do not by chance, but because everything in their lives has led them to do it. To understand Stieg's work, I said, one had to know who he really was. Then I showed the black-and-white photos of his childhood with his grandparents, and the later ones in color of the kitchen with the single cookstove and the grandfather's workshop, where he repaired bicycles, among other things. I explained that to Stieg, these people, poor and culturally marginalized, represented a minority victimized by discrimination. And that in the end, at one moment or another, we can all become such a minority and even, at the whim of history, find ourselves in deadly danger. I spoke of the Danish and Swedish internment camps (Storsien, in northern Sweden, in particular), the deportation of their prisoners, and the fortress of Theresienstadt where the internees were executed or sent on to Auschwitz or other extermination camps. I supplied dates, the numbers of prisoners and of those who perished—all information I had dug up that morning. Then, returning to a picture of Stieg as a baby with his grandfather, I revealed that Stieg had told me Severin Boström had been imprisoned in Storsien, but had miraculously survived to continue the voyage of his life and take care of a little boy who had loved him as his father. Stieg's deep political engagement sprang from his childhood, from such experiences as listening to his grandfather talk about what had happened on Kristallnacht.

I went on to speak about the foundation I wanted to create in memory of Stieg. The idea was to award a prize every year to honor a militant journalist or photographer. I showed one of Stieg's favorite portraits, the photo I'd taken of him from a low angle, in which he's leaning back in the sunlight, squinting and smiling—at me. Beneath the photo, I'd added something taken from an editorial for the December 1997 issue of *Expo*, which never appeared: "We know that what we do is necessary. . . ."

Finally, I concluded by explaining that *Expo* had almost died back in those days, that there'd been no more private funding to keep it afloat and the editorial staff had been exhausted. I hoped everyone now understood why Stieg had used the word "necessary."

I WAS pleased to have been able to carry on throughout that terrible day. To have been able, surrounded by the warmth of our friends, to speak calmly, without being overwhelmed by grief.

This November 9 has been a day not of mourning, but of great spirituality.

◙

Wednesday, November 23
A NEW letter from Erland and Joakim's lawyer. He asks me to sign the enclosed joint agreement regarding the division of the estate, in which it is stipulated that their half of the apartment will be given to me in exchange for my handing Stieg's computer over to them.

In the accompanying letter, the lawyer points out that the Larssons—as well as various people at Norstedts—are unhappy at not having been invited to the gathering commemorating the anniversary of Stieg's death. He mentions my speech, which, they feel, focused only on Stieg's life as a writer.

What a complete misunderstanding of Stieg's commitments! That evening was always a part of Stieg's life. It would have been trivial and unimaginable for Stieg or any other speaker that night to have talked about anything other than the monstrous events of that Night of Broken Glass in 1938. Those who see Stieg solely as an author of crime fiction have never truly known him.

▣

Friday, November 25

AT AROUND seven thirty, the delivery from Ikea was waiting for me at home. Beds, mattresses, sheets, pillowcases, and duvet covers . . . all there!

Went straight back out to buy the caster wheels for the beds in a store in Fridhemsplan, on Kungsholmen. Not the ones I'd planned on, since the holes turned out to be too near the edge, but similar ones, gray, instead of the taller, more slender ones of black wood that I had envisioned.

▣

Saturday, November 26

I WENT to fetch my drill at a friend's house. To drill the holes, I have to clamp the feet in the workbench vise and use a 3.5 mm bit and 4 mm screws. I quickly realized I'd have to gauge the measurements with a longer screw I found in a drawer. I began attaching the feet to the first bed frame, which I installed in the "new" room. Mattress, duvet and pillowcases, satin sheets in black, white, gray, and ocher checks. I rolled the daybed over near the window and settled onto it with cushions at my back to watch Lake Mälaren flow quietly below through the Hammarby Canal. I sat there, in silence and tranquility, for a long while.

I put together and finished the second daybed and set it at an angle along the wall, facing the first one. Perfect. Now I have a room that matches my new life. An office for work, a living room where my guests can relax after dinner, and a guest room for friends passing through. I arranged Stieg's books on teak shelves near the window.

And then I slept there. Slept very well. All those books around me made me feel as if I were sleeping at the center of a benevolent world.

▣

December

AT SOME point in December, Joakim phoned Britt to tell her, among other things, that if I published the fourth volume, Norstedts would not publish the second and third ones [whether Norstedts were aware of this conversation, I do not know].

Britt explained to him that the computer supposedly containing more of the *Millennium* saga was the property of *Expo*, not Stieg. Clearly, this computer has become an obsession for the Larssons! A few days later, their lawyer wrote to *Expo* to find out where the computer was. (This question would be raised at the *Expo* board meeting in January 2006, and the answer, delivered at the end of that same month, would be: "We don't know.")

Expecting to be driven at any moment from my apartment, I began packing my belongings in cardboard boxes. I'm handling the situation well, though, and there isn't anything anymore that's too painful for me to consider or imagine. I've recovered my balance and my inner compass. My therapist even says that I'm making particularly rapid progress.

◙

IT'S TIME to write the epilogue for this year just past. First, though, I must compose a summary of my life with Stieg. I cry as I write "I was loved" because, in the end, that's the only thing that counts.

◙

AFTER ONE year
I wait for a call that never comes
His number in my cell phone
I wait for a smile I never get
His photo on my wall
I wait for a caress I never feel
His jacket in my closet
But I hear his voice answer me
When my despair is at its worst.

◙

WHEN STIEG died, I had but one objective, as I wrote on a piece of paper: "To survive." For 2006, I write these words: "To learn how to live again."

2005–2010

UNTIL 2007, I continued to work regularly with *Expo*. My chief occupations were selecting authors for the website devoted to Stieg and translating any articles that were in English. At first, I often worked at the office to show that I wasn't abandoning the magazine, but I also went there because I needed to distract myself from missing Stieg. His death prodded many people's consciences, so *Expo*'s financial situation had considerably improved: beginning in November 2004, spontaneous donations started coming in, and in early 2005 the Förening artister mot nazister (Association of Artists Against Nazis) committed itself for six years to an annual contribution of 500,000 kronor ($72,000). In addition, the Statens Kulturåd

(National Council of Culture) was now providing financial aid for the magazine's printing costs, and *Expo* had begun a long-term collaboration with the publishing firm Natur & Kultur.

My last contribution to the magazine and the foundation was to renovate the office in 2007. Since the budget was barely 30,000 kronor (a little over $4,000), I spent three months washing and repainting the walls and ceilings, which were in poor shape. I wanted a warm shade for the floor, so I picked a dark red. For everything else, I used black and white, "newspaper" colors. I also built a conference table with some salvaged materials. The net effect is rather sober and spare, except for the archives room, where folders and old newspapers are piled up ad infinitum.

Today, a representative of *Expo* serves on the jury for the Stieg Larsson Prize, an award organized by the Larsson family and the Norstedts Publishing Group.

Expo has survived and follows its path. I will follow mine.

◉

SINCE AUTUMN 2007, my apartment in Stockholm has belonged to me free and clear. Almost three years after Stieg's death, the Larssons suddenly had the official papers delivered to me. Until then, I'd been left hanging, ready at a moment's notice to abandon ship, so for two years I'd been living surrounded by cardboard boxes. At last relieved of uncertainty, I unpacked my things and threw a big housewarming party, inviting everyone who'd stood by me through thick and thin. Nowadays, books are taking up more and more room in my six hundred square feet of space and will soon start feeling crowded. Not me! I've repainted the walls here and had a new kitchen put in, white and olive green. The apartment no longer resembles what it was when Stieg lived here. I could no longer bear opening my front door onto our former life, where the slightest detail reminded me that he was gone. I also bought a secondhand oriental rug for the living room, cheap: it was dirty and damaged, but it's a Kashgai woven by one of the craftswomen of that nomadic Iranian tribe. On it is a garden full of trees and flowers, with some ducks, I believe, strolling around in the greenery. After washing and mending the rug, I laid it on the floor, put on a little music, and danced the salsa barefoot on this new realm. I felt in my body that the apartment had become mine, and that my home had lost that painful echo of happy times lost forever.

▣

I RETURNED to my professional life in the building industry, still in the domain of sustainable development. This is my world. A hard and demanding world, but a fair one. My work has meaning because it acts on reality. I can use my skills freely and make decisions I find effective. This isn't the virtual reality of the *Millennium* industry, where I can't decide anything at all.

This *Millennium* industry was born in July 2005, seven months after Stieg died, when *Men Who Hate Women* (in English: *The Girl with the Dragon Tattoo*) came out in Sweden, and it has become a juggernaut with the success of the trilogy: more than forty million books have been sold to this date throughout the world, not to mention the audiobooks and the films for TV and the cinema. Along with this industry, a myth has sprung up: the *Millennium* Stieg. Everything under the sun has since been written and said about him. And usually by people who barely knew him, knew nothing of our life, and shared none of our struggles. Why? Because Stieg and I were never celebrities, never got the red-carpet treatment at evening premieres, never had the *New York Times*, *Le Monde*, the *Guardian*, or *El País* clamoring to interview us the way they do now to talk to me about Stieg and the trilogy. Stieg's real life, like mine, was often boring, always hardworking, and sometimes dangerous. That's why those people who today have so much to say about him never came anywhere near us.

▣

THE MILLENNIUM Trilogy is not just a good story made up by a good author of good crime novels. These books talk about the need to fight to defend one's ideals, and the refusal to give up, to sell oneself, or to grovel before someone powerful. The novels speak of values, justice, of journalism in the noble sense of the word, of the integrity and efficiency some people bring to their jobs, including the police. The novels talk about morality, too. The virtual reality that has overtaken Stieg today has cast him as the hero of the trilogy. Well, Stieg didn't wait for the *Millennium* books to be what he was. And in that reductive vision of Stieg, certain people have even tried to erase me from the map—along with our thirty-two years together! Unfortunately, this attitude is fueled in part by misogyny, and not just toward me: wherever the myth of Stieg Larsson is involved, women are always devalued, whereas he collaborated mostly with women all his life. In April 2007, my sister told me she'd just noticed that someone had changed the Wikipedia entry on Stieg: ever since November 18, 2006, the site now said that he had never lived with his grandparents, but always with his mother and father! And where the text had previously said that Eva Gabrielsson was his lifelong partner at the time of his death, now it read: "with whom he was living periodically at the time of his death." The link with my interview on the problems with his estate, which had appeared in *Attention*, an economic journal, had also been removed.

◙

SOMEWHERE AROUND 2006, the foreign media began to take an interest in the man behind *The Millennium Trilogy*, at first in the Scandinavian countries, then in Europe. Now members of the media from the United States and

Australia come to Stockholm to talk to me about Stieg. They assume—correctly—that I must be the person with the most interesting things to say, after three decades of life with him.

◻

THE JOURNALISTS invariably ask the same questions, in the same order. The first one comes out like clockwork: Does everything shown in the trilogy (corruption, abuses of power, discrimination and violence against women, etc.) really exist in Sweden?

When I reply that most of the facts, events, and characters are real, the journalists are astounded. It's strange that Sweden always seems like a model to many other nations, when here we have the same problems found everywhere else. These interviews show me that the trilogy has taken some of the luster off Sweden's image as a progressive and egalitarian model for human rights.

The second question is rooted in the journalists' astonishment that I am not considered Stieg's widow after all those years spent together. How can our country allow such a situation to exist? A good question.

The Millennium Trilogy is today one of the most important Swedish exports, with—I repeat—more than forty million copies sold worldwide. But the trilogy is more than a few books: it's a phenomenon that has had two major effects. The first is to have allowed a new image of Sweden to spread all over the globe. The second is that Stieg and the trilogy have become a kind of merchandise that can be endlessly commercialized.

◨

THAT IS why I asked to be put in charge of Stieg's literary estate. Every offer made by my lawyers since 2006 has reflected that wish. Every offer has left the Larssons free to choose the percentage of royalties assigned to me in payment for such work, which would thus allow them to remain the beneficiaries of most of the revenues. A long silence would always follow each of our offers . . . until their NO arrived. My lawyer, Sara Pers-Krause, summed things up for the Swedish media in November 2009: "We would like to emphasize that the important thing for us is the management of Stieg Larsson's intellectual property and that we have, to this end, presented different requests since the spring of 2006 without ever receiving a single reply to any of our offers."

◨

AFTER FEBRUARY 2009 and all through the summer, the newspapers played up the negotiations between Yellow Bird and Sony's production company in Hollywood over an American adaptation of *The Millennium Trilogy*. Familiar with the moral values of the United States and knowing that, unlike Sweden, twelve American states have laws guaranteeing the inheritance rights of common-law wives, I was curious to see what would happen. I was not disappointed.

▣

ON OCTOBER 25, 2009, the Swedish evening paper *Aftonbladet* called me to discuss an article that would appear on the 26th in the daily *Dagens Nyheter*. Did I have any comment to make regarding the 2 million kronor (about $300,000) the Larssons would be paying me? I replied that I didn't know anything about that, and neither did my lawyer. And nothing was published.

One week later, on November 2, the rival daily *Svenska Dagbladet* explained in its columns that the Larssons were now offering me 20 million kronor (almost $3 million). All I could say was that once again, my lawyer and I had been left out of that loop.

That same day, my lawyer called the Larssons' new lawyer to state clearly that a newspaper article could not be considered a serious offer, and that we expected something more formal. This news made the rounds of the foreign media.

One month later, *Variety* reported in America that "the deal hasn't closed yet; it's been gestating for six months because of a rights dispute between Larsson's parents and his longtime partner, Eva Gabrielsson."

▣

IT WAS at this point that discussion of the management of Stieg's literary estate resumed among the Larssons, our lawyers, and me.

In the course of these negotiations, the Larssons offered me a seat on the board of their company, which administers the revenues generated by *The Millennium Trilogy*. This position would have given me access to contracts and financial reports without allowing me any control over how the trilogy and Stieg's political writings were used. His intellectual property could be sold, rewritten, changed—and my role would have been that of a simple consultant, heeded or ignored at will by the two owners of the company.

In April 2010, my lawyer offered a compromise: I would have the right to manage "the other texts," meaning everything but *The Millennium Trilogy*. And we waited for an answer.

◫

IN MAY 2010, a book I'd written with Gunnar von Sydow was published: *Sambo: ensammare än du tror* (*Concubine: More Alone Than You Think*). In January 2008, I'd begun to wonder if my predicament might be more common than I thought: cohabitation without benefit of marriage is widespread in Sweden, so many people must have been in my position, and in the course of my research I naturally discovered many men and women who were my companions in misfortune. My coauthor and I found out something astonishing, however: our most solid arguing point—the significant number of couples involved—vanished in a flash! As it turns out, we are all only a *minority* for the government, since the National Swedish Institute of Statistics only counts couples *who have children together*. Everyone else is classified as "single."*

□

SIX weeks after our compromise offer was made, Joakim and Erland Larsson replied simultaneously, via a press release and an email to my lawyer, that they were breaking off negotiations with me.

□

FIAT JUSTITIA, pereat mundus. Let justice be done, though all the world perish.

---

* Sweden is one of the first countries to have tried to regulate the situation of unmarried partners by passing a law of minimal protection for the "weakest" partner: division of the home in 1973, and of community property in 1987. In 2003, these rights were extended to homosexual couples living together.

Today this law is clearly most useful to couples who separate. When one partner dies intestate, the surviving partner falls into a legal black hole—unlike the situation faced by a married couple, where the survivor inherits automatically unless a will stipulates otherwise. So, when two people live together without being married or having children and one partner dies intestate, the legal problems of inheritance are worked out amicably.

Or not. In France, for example, ever since 1999 a *pacte civil de solidarité*, a legal form of civil union, has granted inheritance rights to the surviving partner if there is a will to this effect, or if a declaration was made when the PACS was registered stipulating that all property acquired after the date of the PACS would be held in common. (*Sambo: ensammare än du tror*, Eva Gabrielsson and Gunnar von Sydow, Blue Publishing, 2010.)

supporteva.com

EARLY IN April 2009, my lawyer received an unexpected request from a former journalist, Jan M. Moberg (at the time the director general of the Norwegian media group Edda Media), and his lawyer.

Jan M. Moberg had just seen a rebroadcast of "The Millennium Millions," a special report on Swedish television on how Stieg's father and brother had come by his estate. During that program, the Larssons had mentioned that one of their ideas for "solving the problem" had been that I should marry Stieg's father.

Jan M. Moberg and two of his friends, roused to indignation, wanted to launch a website—www.supporteva.com—that would bring me some moral and financial support.

Calling themselves the Three Musketeers of Drammen, they saw their creation of this site as an application of the same philosophy of action and justice that animates the trilogy. Their objective was to collect money and open an account for me on the Internet, administered by their lawyer in Norway. I was pleasantly surprised by their professionalism, and my lawyer gave me the go-ahead to accept their offer.

◉

THESE NORWEGIANS seem to have a particularly delightful sense of humor. The website, which was launched within three weeks and translated into several languages, invites Internauts to contribute a sum commensurate with the number of Stieg's novels they have read and their degree of outrage over my predicament. On the Comments page, messages of encouragement come in from around the world, and I've received as many phone calls and emails from perfect strangers as I have from my own friends and acquaintances, all telling me that they were relieved to finally have a way to tell me publicly how they felt.

◉

RIGHT BEFORE the site went online, Erland and Joakim Larsson donated 4 million kronor (a little less than $600,000) to *Expo*, on top of a previous gift of 1 million kronor (not quite $150,000). This news prompted the Norwegians to contact *Expo* and *Searchlight*, the two biggest antifascist magazines for which Stieg had written, to ask them to write about the site and publicize a link to it. The British magazine immediately allocated a large space on its website to this end. *Expo*, however, replied that my conflict with the Larssons was unfortunate, but that they couldn't take sides in a private matter. The same point was raised by Norstedts, which declined to help.

⊡

ON MAY 25, 2009, Norstedts and the Larssons together awarded their first "Stieg Larsson Prize" of 200,000 kronor, almost $30,000, in memory of Stieg's battles against injustice.

It was presented to *Expo*.

The Fourth Volume

AS I'VE already related, my sister Britt went with Erland to *Expo*'s office on the morning after Stieg's death, and I asked her to take my partner's backpack along with her. It contained his agenda, with booked lectures, meetings and deadlines, the detailed outline for the next issue, and the *Expo* laptop. This computer thus belongs to the magazine, but it also contains Stieg's articles, his correspondence with *Searchlight*, his research, the names of his informants, etc. For this reason, the laptop is protected by the Swedish Constitution's Freedom of the Press Act, which says that a journalist's sources must be kept confidential. This computer, unprotected by any secret password, remained in the *Expo* office for more than six months. At the time, someone suggested that it be put in the office safe, but the safe was locked and only Stieg knew the combination!

The laptop contains the fourth volume of the *Millennium* saga . . . perhaps.

This text is a little more than two hundred pages long, because when we went on vacation that last summer, Stieg had already written more than a hundred and sixty pages. Between going over the first volume a few times in the final editing, finishing the third one, and his work at *Expo*, Stieg probably didn't have time in the weeks before his death to add more than fifty pages to the fourth volume.

I have no intention of summarizing here the plot of the fourth novel. I would like to say, however, that in this book Lisbeth Salander gradually breaks free of all of her ghosts and enemies. Every time she manages to take revenge on someone who has harmed her, physically or psychologically, she has the tattoo symbolizing that person removed. Lisbeth's piercings are her way of following the fashion of others her age, but those tattoos are her war paint. To some extent, the young woman behaves like a native in an urban jungle, acting like an animal, relying on instinct, of course, but always on the alert as well for what may lie ahead, sniffing out danger. Like Lisbeth, I trust my instincts when I encounter new people and situations. As Stieg well knew.

In the space of two years, Stieg wrote two thousand pages of the trilogy, almost without notes or research (except for small details). How did he do it? Simple: the basic material for these books is our personal lives and our thirty-two years together. The trilogy is the fruit of Stieg's experience, but of mine as well. Rooted in Stieg's childhood, but in mine, too. Rooted in our battles, our commitments, our trips, our passions, our fears. . . . These books are the jigsaw puzzle of our lives. That's why I cannot tell exactly what part of *The Millennium Trilogy* comes from Stieg and what comes from me. What I *can* say is that if anyone ever decided to take up the challenge to continue the adventure, each book would require years of work.

The vicissitudes of life arranged for Stieg, not me, to bring all of those things together to create literature. Ironically, some people insist that I made no contribution whatsoever to the trilogy—while others claim that I wrote the whole thing. I can only say that just as Stieg and I shared a common language, we often wrote together.

In August 2005, Per-Erik Nilsson submitted an offer to the Larssons and to Norstedts in which he asked that I be given control of the moral rights to Stieg's work. That way I would have been able to work legally on his texts and finish the fourth book, which I am capable of doing. My lawyer felt that this prospect would inspire the Larssons to find a solution to our impasse.

The Larssons said no.

It should be made clear here that nothing in Swedish inheritance law obliges anyone to inherit a legacy. No one is prevented from giving away all or part of an inheritance. The law also allows the moral rights to an author's oeuvre to be transferred to someone else.

Stieg's and my situation—and that of many other couples I mention in my book on unmarried partners, where the surviving companion loses everything after the other one dies—shows that these archaic laws must change, because they treat intellectual creations as if they were plots of land to be added to the relatives' nearby farmland. When one unmarried partner dies, the other is abruptly stripped of all the couple has built up together, and is thereby prevented from developing their joint creation. And when this legacy is handed over to people who have had nothing to do with it, this is not only immoral but also detrimental to the creative elements in society, since it's the passive who win and the active who lose. Which means that society stagnates. This unfair situation, publicized through my case, has led many people in Sweden to make their domestic union legally safer, sometimes through marriage.

◙

WITHOUT THE support of our true friends—who do not camp out on TV soundstages, trotting out apocryphal memories and bizarre stories about Stieg for the media or in books—I would never have made it through these last years. This book is also my thanks to them.

Today I'm still fighting to control the literary rights to *The Millennium Trilogy* and all of Stieg's political writing. I'm fighting for him, for me, for us.

I do not want his name to be an industry or a brand. The way things are going, what's to stop me from one day seeing his name on a bottle of beer, a packet of coffee, or a car? I don't want his struggles and ideals to be sullied and exploited. I know how he would react in every situation I'm facing today: he would fight.

Like Stieg, that's what I must do.

On the evening of Stieg's burial, I wrote that I wanted "to survive another year." A few months later, on the anniversary of his death, I hoped "to learn how to live again." Today, the words I calmly write are . . . "to live." My family, my work, my commitments, my friends: they are what lets me live each and every day.

For Stieg. Because he would ask that of me, the way he did in his farewell letter before he set out for Africa in 1977 when he was twenty-two.

So for me, for us, and because that's the way we are, I will keep going.

Acknowledgments

Marie-Françoise Colombani would like to thank:
Eva Gabrielsson, for her trust
Régis Boyer, specialist in Scandinavian literature and
civilization, and Gunnar Lund, the Swedish ambas-
sador to France, for their valuable assistance
H. Poussin, for his support and ornithological expertise
Michelle Fitoussi, an early and devoted fan of
The Millennium Trilogy, for her knowledge of building
construction and Bruno Lafforgue for his patience.